Teaching Pal 2

Authors and Advisors

Alma Flor Ada • Kylene Beers • F. Isabel Campoy
Joyce Armstrong Carroll • Nathan Clemens
Anne Cunningham • Martha Hougen
Elena Izquierdo • Carol Jago • Erik Palmer
Robert Probst • Shane Templeton • Julie Washington

Contributing Consultants

David Dockterman • Mindset Works
Jill Eggleton

Printed in the U.S.A.

ISBN 978-1-328-51712-8

2 3 4 5 6 7 8 9 10 0607 27 26 25 24 23 22 21 20 19 18

4500720031 A B C D E F G

Navigating the Teaching Pal

The Teaching Pal is a companion to the Teacher's Guide, providing point-of-use instructional notes for using the student texts in *my*Book for different purposes.

Blue Notes
READ FOR UNDERSTANDING

During a first reading of the complete text, use these notes to guide collaborative discussion about the gist of the text.

 READ FOR UNDERSTANDING

ASK: Why is Dilly alone? *(Possible responses: Minna could not swim as fast as Dilly; Dilly was having so much fun, he didn't think about where he was going.)*

ANNOTATION TIP: Have children underline the words that tell how Dilly feels.

FOLLOW-UP: What do you think Dilly will do? *(Accept reasonable responses.)*

DOK 2

Purple Notes
TARGETED CLOSE READ

During subsequent readings, use these notes to take a closer look at sections of the text to apply a reading skill.

 TARGETED CLOSE READ

Characters

Have children reread pages 70–71 to identify the story characters.

ASK: Who are the characters in the story? *(two friends, Dilly and Minna)*

FOLLOW-UP: What do you know about them? *(Dilly looks different from Minna and the other ducks; Dilly and Minna like to have fun together.)*

ANNOTATION TIP: Have children underline the words that describe Dilly.

DOK 3

Yellow Notes

Use these notes for teaching support on the pages that appear before and after each text.

Academic Discussion

Use the TURN AND TALK routine. Remind children to follow agreed-upon rules for discussion, such as taking turns speaking and adding to their partner's ideas.

Possible responses:

- *Why was Dilly bigger than the other ducks? Would Dilly ever see Minna again?* DOK 1
- *Even though Dilly looks different, he is still special.* DOK 2

Red Notes
NOTICE & NOTE

Use these notes to help children learn to look for signposts in a text in order to create meaning.

Notice & Note

Contrasts and Contradictions

Remind children that when a character acts or feels differently than we expect, the author is showing us something important about the character.

Tell them that when that happens, they should stop to notice and note, which includes asking themselves questions about what they read.

Have children explain why they might use this strategy on pages 72–73. *(Dilly was always happy, but now he is sad and afraid.)*

Remind them of the Anchor Question: **Why might Dilly feel this way?** *(He is alone and lost.)*

DOK 2

TABLE OF CONTENTS

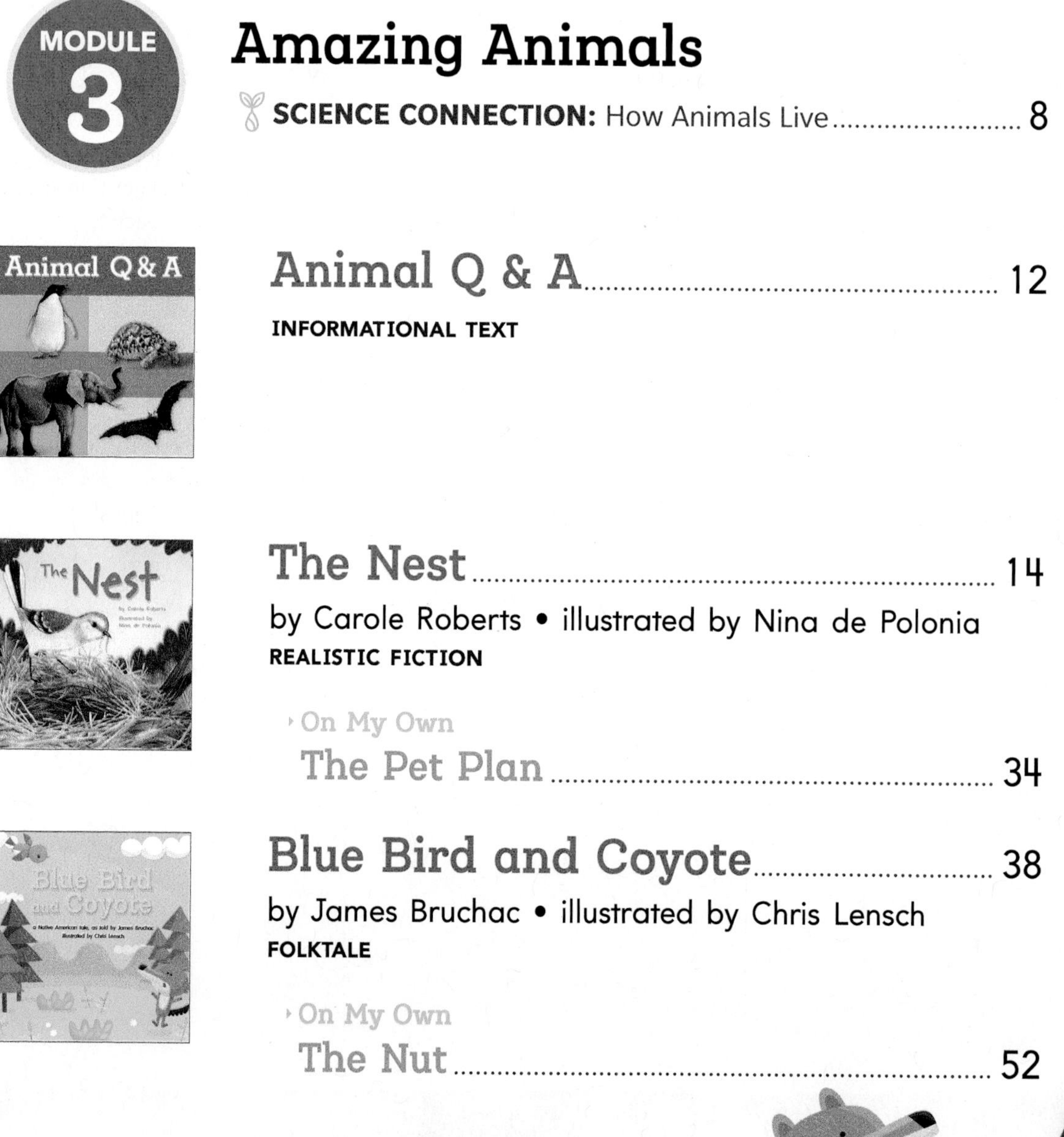

Amazing Animals

Better Together

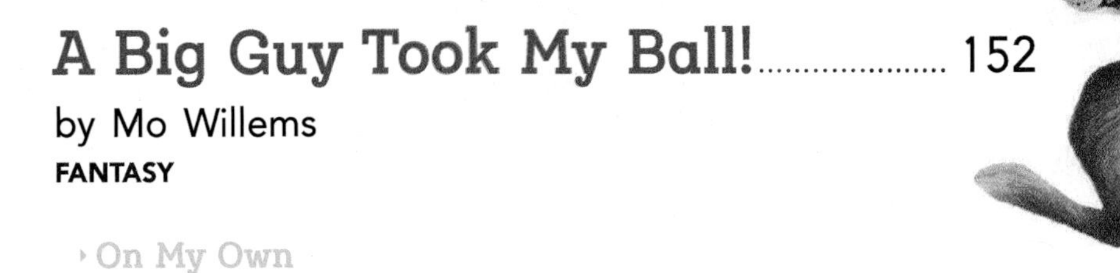

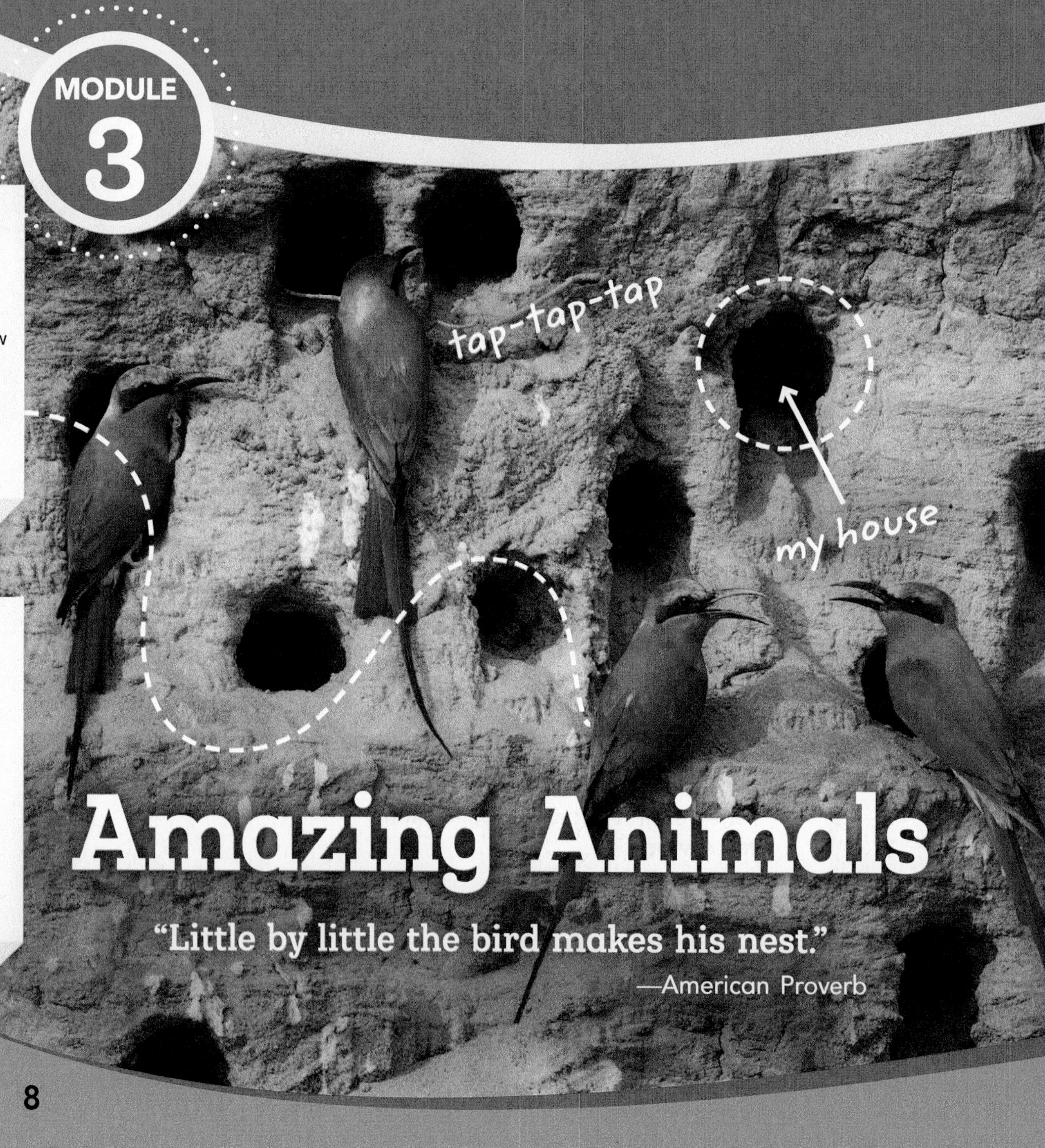

Introduce the Topic

- **Read aloud** the module title, *Amazing Animals.*
- **Tell children** that in this module they will be reading texts about how animals live.
- **Have children** share prior knowledge about the topic or word associations for how animals live. Record their ideas in a web.

Discuss the Quotation

- **Read aloud** the American proverb.
- **Lead a discussion** in which children try to explain the quote in their own words. Explain the meaning as needed: *A big job becomes easier if you do it step by step.*

ASK: What types of jobs are easier to do step by step? *(Accept reasonable responses.)*

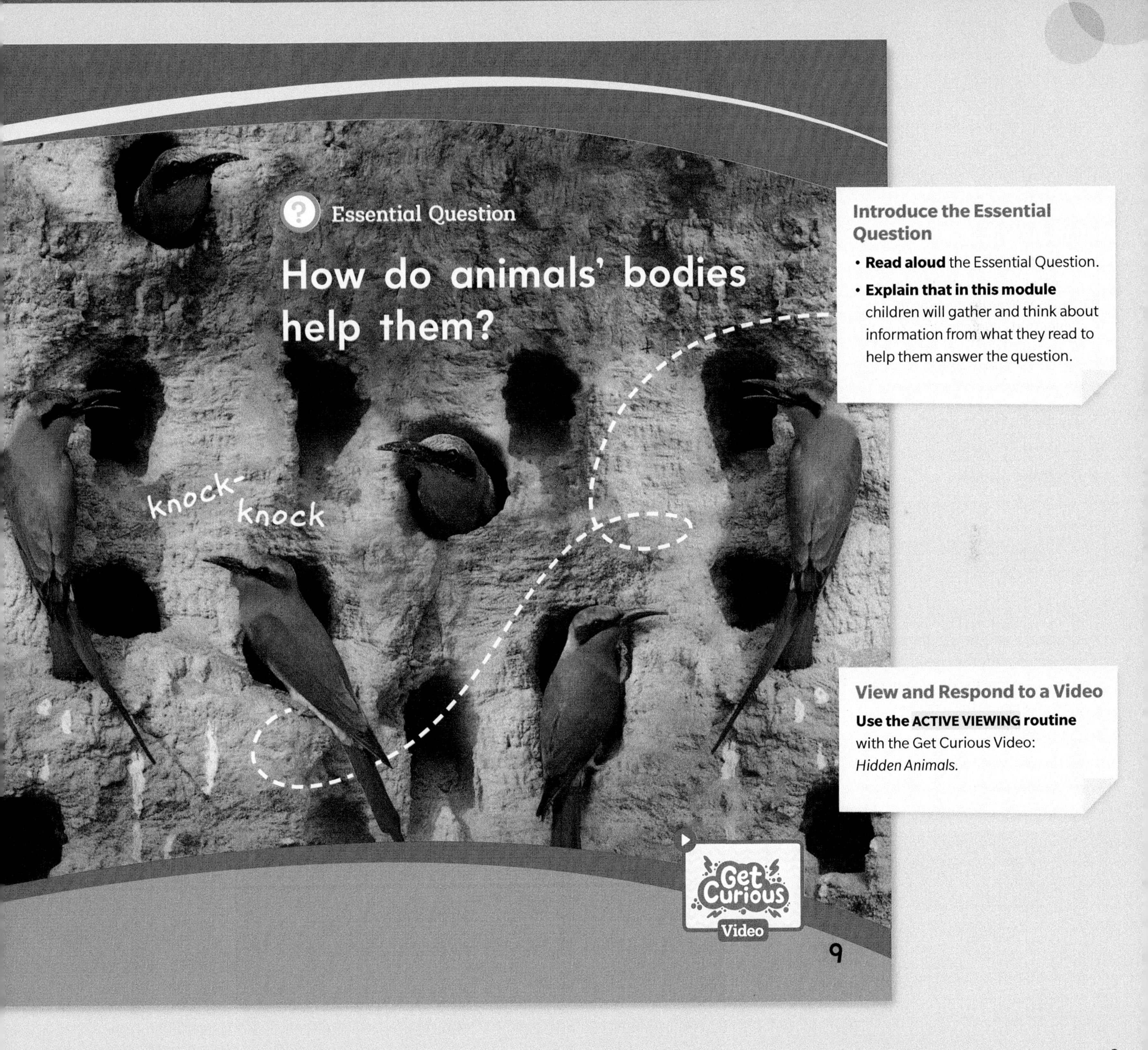

Introduce the Essential Question

- **Read aloud** the Essential Question.
- **Explain that in this module** children will gather and think about information from what they read to help them answer the question.

View and Respond to a Video

Use the ACTIVE VIEWING routine with the Get Curious Video: *Hidden Animals.*

Big Idea Words

Use the VOCABULARY routine and the Vocabulary Cards to introduce the Big Idea Words *camouflage, mammal,* and *characteristics*. You may wish to display the corresponding Vocabulary Card for each word as you discuss it.

1. Say the Big Idea Word.
2. Explain the meaning.
3. Talk about examples.

Vocabulary Network

- **Encourage children** to think about animals whose fur or coloring can easily blend into the environment as they complete the activity for *camouflage*.

Words About How Animals Live

Complete the Vocabulary Network to show what you know about the words.

camouflage

Meaning: **Camouflage** is what hides something or makes it difficult to see.

Synonyms and Antonyms	Drawing

10

mammal

Meaning: A **mammal** is a kind of animal that has hair and feeds milk to its babies.

Synonyms and Antonyms	Drawing

characteristics

Meaning: **Characteristics** are things that make a person, animal, or thing different from others.

Synonyms and Antonyms	Drawing

Vocabulary Network

- **As children complete** the activity for *mammal,* prompt them to think of pets and wild animals they are familiar with.
- **Ask children** to think about the *characteristics* of different mammals as they complete the activity.

Short Read

READ Together

Animal Q & A

Imagine that *you* had wings! What could *you* do? Find out what animals can do with *their* bodies!

READ FOR UNDERSTANDING

Introduce the Text

- **Read aloud** the title, *Animal Q&A*. Tell children that it is an informational text. Ask them to recall what they know about informational texts. *(They contain facts about a topic.)*
- Guide children to **set a purpose.**
- **Read the text** with children.

DOK 3

READ FOR UNDERSTANDING

Text Features

- **ASK: How does the author use italic and bold text?** *(to call attention to important words in the text)*

ANNOTATION TIP: Have children underline the words in italics and circle the words in bold.

DOK 2

Q: What could you do with **wings?**

A: **Swim!** Penguins flap to go fast!

Q: What could you do with a **shell?**

A: **Hide!** Turtles are safe inside.

12

Q: What could you do with a **trunk?**

A: **Snorkel!** Elephants get air like this.

Q: What could you do with **claws?**

A: **Grab!** Bats hang upside down to sleep.

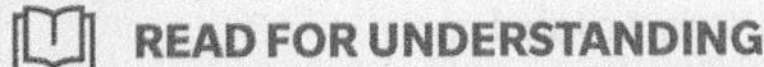

READ FOR UNDERSTANDING

Text Features

ASK: What else does the author do to call attention to important information in the text? *(Possible response: The author uses different size text to label the photos.)*

FOLLOW-UP: What information do the labels give? *(The labels give clues to help you answer the questions.)*

DOK 2

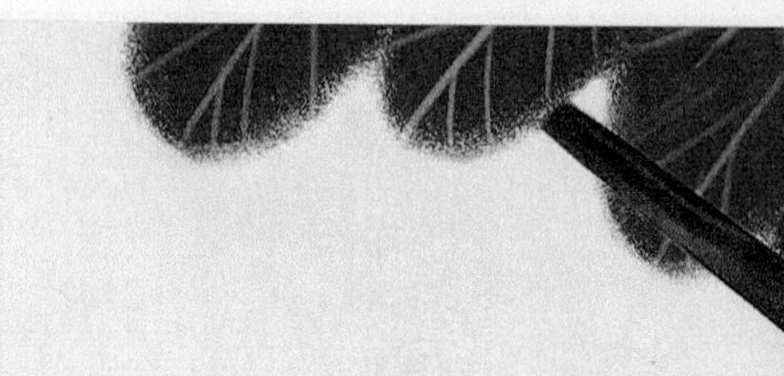

READ FOR UNDERSTANDING

Introduce the Text

- **Read aloud** and discuss the information about the genre.
- **Guide children** to set a purpose for reading to practice asking and answering questions.
- **Provide information** about the illustrator, Nina de Polonia.
- **Tell children** to look for and think about the Power Words as they read.

Prepare to Read

GENRE STUDY **Realistic fiction** stories are made up but could happen in real life. Look for:

- characters and a setting that seem real
- ways the pictures and words work together to tell the story

SET A PURPOSE **Ask questions** before, during, and after you read to help you understand the text. Look for evidence in the text and pictures to **answer** your questions.

POWER WORDS
exclaimed
twigs
surprise
soon
warm
empty

Meet Nina de Polonia.

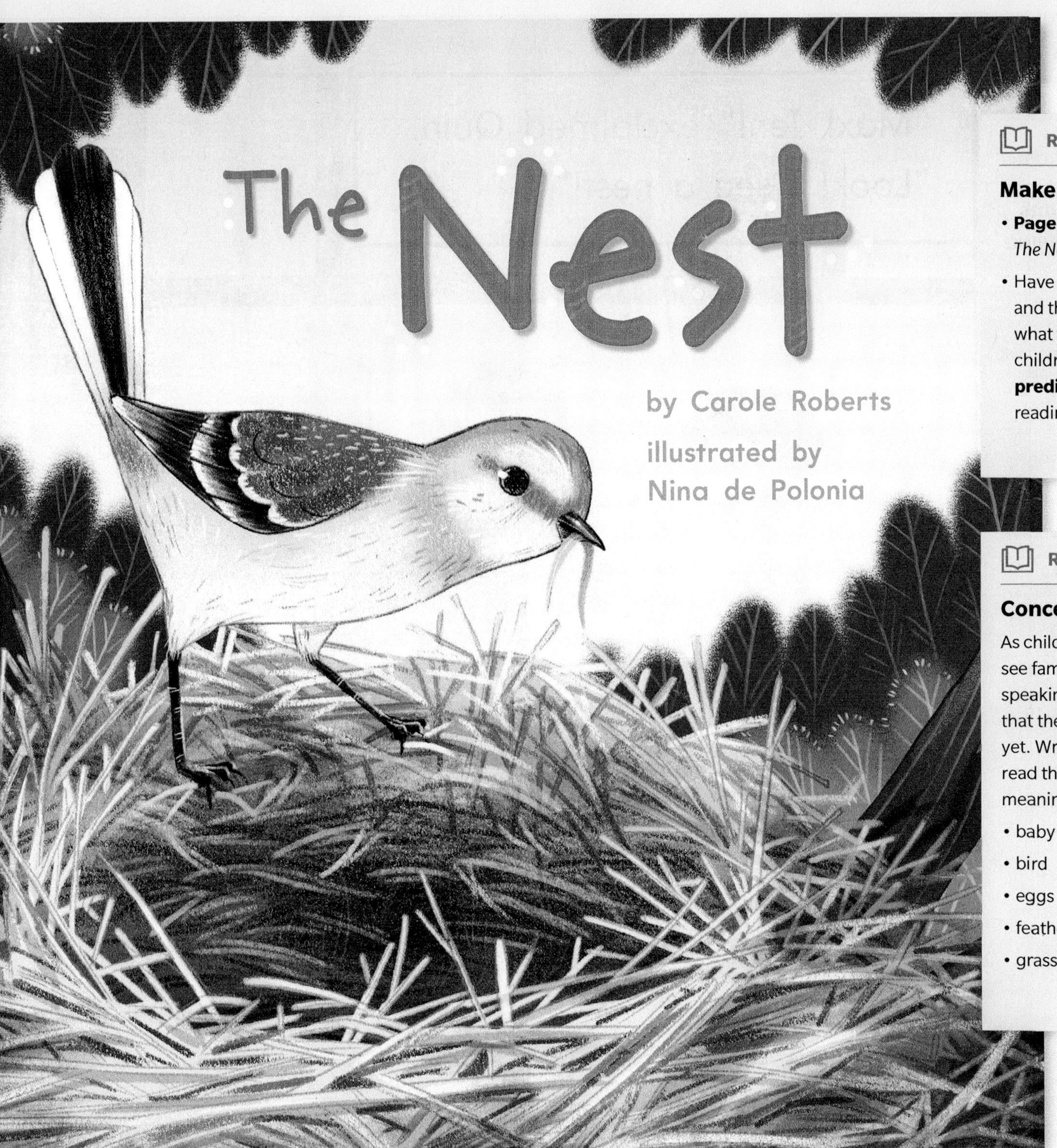

READ FOR UNDERSTANDING

Make Predictions

- **Page through** the beginning of *The Nest* with children.
- Have them **use prior knowledge** and the illustrations to predict what the story will be about. Tell children they will **return to their predictions** after they finish reading the story.

DOK 2

READ FOR UNDERSTANDING

Concept Words

As children read *The Nest,* they may see familiar words from their speaking and listening vocabularies that they may not know how to read yet. Write these words on the board, read them aloud, and discuss their meanings as needed.

- baby
- bird
- eggs
- feathers
- grass
- leaves
- mockingbird
- paper
- soft

DOK 2

READ FOR UNDERSTANDING

Ask and Answer Questions

MODEL ASKING AND ANSWERING A QUESTION

THINK ALOUD *Before I read, I ask questions that help me put into words things that I am curious about. When I look at the picture on this page, I ask myself: Where are the children? What is the girl pointing to? I will look for answers to these questions as I read.*

DOK 2

TARGETED CLOSE READ

Story Structure

Have children reread pages 16–19 to analyze the story's structure.

ASK: What happens at the beginning of the story? *(The children see a bird building a nest outside.)*

DOK 1

17

READ FOR UNDERSTANDING

ASK: Where do the children see a nest? *(in a tree outside their classroom)*

FOLLOW-UP: How do you know? *(The picture shows the children inside a classroom, looking out the window at a bird's nest in a tree.)*

DOK 2

READ FOR UNDERSTANDING

Phonics/Decoding in Context

Have children point to the word *Quin*. Review that the letters *qu* together stand for the sound /kw/. **Model blending** the sounds in the word: /kw/ /ĭ/ /n/, *Quin*. Have children repeat. Point out that *Quin* is a name and names begin with a capital letter.

ANNOTATION TIP: Have children use what they know about words that name people and capital letters to find and circle all the names on the page.

READ FOR UNDERSTANDING

Ask and Answer Questions

ASK: What questions might you have while reading this page? *(Possible responses: What kind of bird is a mockingbird? What is the mockingbird doing in the nest? Why does it build a nest?)*

FOLLOW-UP: How can you answer your questions? *(Possible responses: I can keep reading; I can look for details in the text and photos.)*

DOK 2

READ FOR UNDERSTANDING

Quick Teach Words

As needed to support comprehension, briefly explain the meaning of *Mrs.* in this context.

- *Mrs.* is a word used as a title for a woman who is married.

ANNOTATION TIP: Have children circle the teacher's complete name and read it together.

19

READ FOR UNDERSTANDING

ASK: How does the bird make the nest? *(It weaves twigs and grass together.)*

FOLLOW-UP: How do you know? *(The words say the nest is made of twigs and grass; the pictures show the bird adding twigs and grass to the nest.)*

DOK 3

"The grass will make it soft," said Ben.

 **READ FOR UNDERSTANDING**

Phonics/Decoding in Context

Have children point to the words *Ben* and *Wes*. Review that when there is only one vowel in a word and it is followed by a consonant, it usually stands for its short vowel sound. **Model blending** the sounds in each name: /b/ /ĕ/ /n/, *Ben*; /w/ /ĕ/ /s/, *Wes*. Have children repeat.

ANNOTATION TIP: Have children label each of the characters.

"I see twigs and leaves," said Wes.

"I see bits of paper," said Liz.

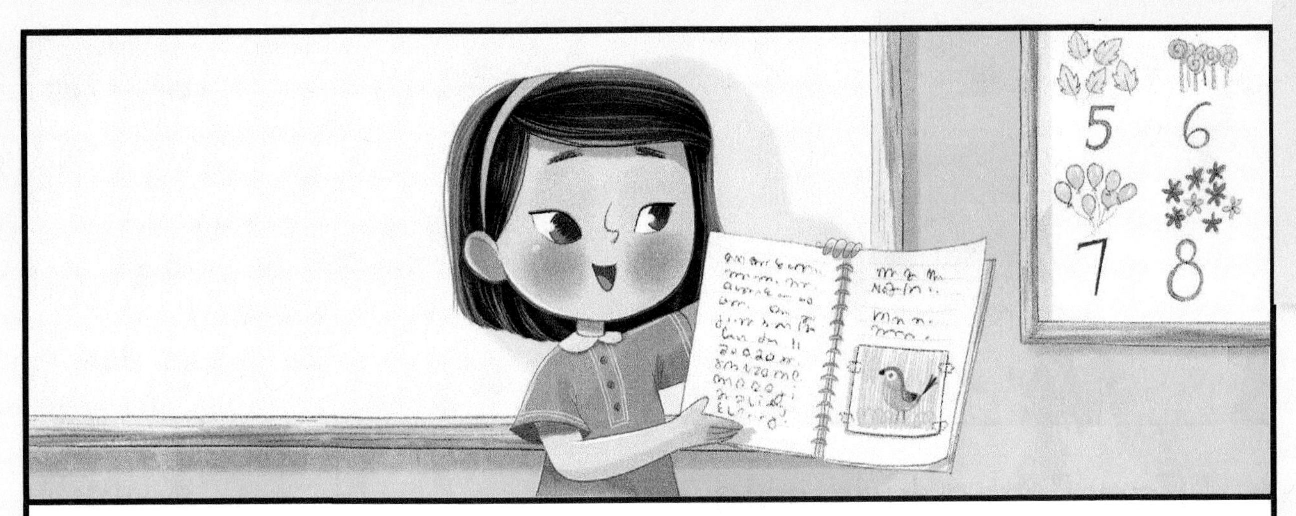

"We can write about it!" said Jen.

READ FOR UNDERSTANDING

ASK: What do you think Jen wrote about in her journal? *(Possible response: She wrote about the bird and the materials it used to make its nest.)*

ANNOTATION TIP: Have children underline the words on pages 20–21 that tell what the nest is made of.

FOLLOW-UP: Have you ever written a journal entry or a report about something you saw? *(Accept reasonable responses.)*

DOK 2

READ FOR UNDERSTANDING

Ask and Answer Questions

MODEL ASKING AND ANSWERING A QUESTION

THINK ALOUD *Now I see why the mockingbird built the nest! I wonder what will happen to the eggs? I'll keep reading to see if I can find out the answer to this question.*

DOK 2

22

"We will look at the nest every day," said Mrs. Web.

"Will we see baby birds?" asked Quin. "Soon?" everyone asked.

READ FOR UNDERSTANDING

Quick Teach Words

As needed to support comprehension, briefly explain the meaning of *everyone* in this context.

- *Everyone* means all of the people in the group. In this story, *everyone* means all of the children in the classroom.

ANNOTATION TIP: Have children circle the two smaller words in the word *everyone*.

Notice & Note

Again and Again

- **Remind children** that if they see a word or picture that is repeated in a story, they should stop to notice and note. Explain that this can help them answer questions they might have about what is happening in the story.
- **Have children explain** why they might use this strategy on page 24. *(The two pictures are almost the same, but one is at night and one is during the day; the word sat is repeated, so that must mean the bird sat for a long time.)*

ANNOTATION TIP: Have children circle the words that repeat.

- **Remind them** of the Anchor Question: **Why might the author say the word *sat* again and again?** *(to show that the bird sat on the eggs for a long time)*

DOK 3

24

One day, the kids see baby birds!

25

TARGETED CLOSE READ

Story Structure

Have children reread pages 25 and 30 to analyze the story's structure.

ASK: What happens in the middle and at the end of the story? *(The baby birds hatch and then fly out of the nest.)*

FOLLOW-UP: Which words help tell when the events happen? *("One day")*

DOK 2

26

READ FOR UNDERSTANDING

Ask and Answer Questions

ASK: What questions might you ask yourself about the baby birds? *(Possible responses: What do the baby birds eat? Can the baby birds fly? What will the baby birds do?)*

FOLLOW-UP: How can you answer your questions? *(Possible responses: I can keep reading; I can look for details in the text and pictures that answer my questions.)*

DOK 2

"Soon they will get big feathers," said Quin.

READ FOR UNDERSTANDING

ASK: How have the baby birds changed? *(They are bigger; they look fluffier; they have more feathers.)*

ANNOTATION TIP: Have children underline the words that describe what the baby birds are like.

DOK 2

28

READ FOR UNDERSTANDING

ASK: How do the baby birds learn to fly? *(Possible responses: Their parents show them how to; they try and try until they can fly.)*

FOLLOW-UP: How do you know? *(The pictures show the big birds showing the baby birds how to fly; the word try is repeated in the text.)*

ANNOTATION TIP: Have children find and circle the word *try* on pages 28–29.

DOK 2

29

READ FOR UNDERSTANDING

ASK: What do you think will happen now that the baby birds can fly? *(Possible responses: They will leave the nest; they will find another place to live.)*

DOK 2

READ FOR UNDERSTANDING

Quick Teach Words

As needed to support comprehension, briefly explain the meaning of *quiet* in this context.

- When it is *quiet*, there is little or no noise.

READ FOR UNDERSTANDING

Wrap Up

Revisit the predictions children made before reading. Have them confirm or correct their predictions using evidence from the text and pictures.

DOK 2

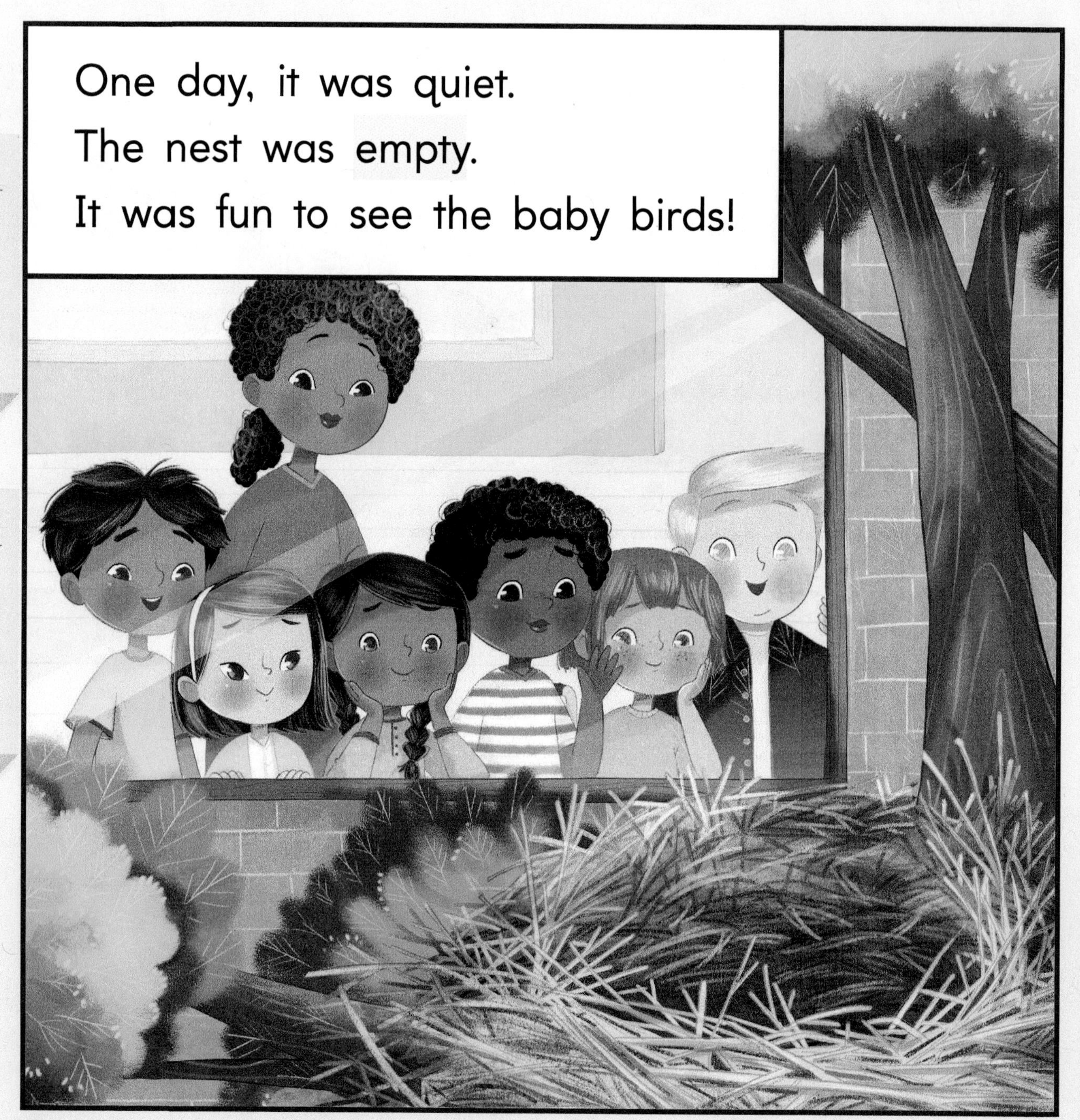

30

Respond to Reading

READ Together

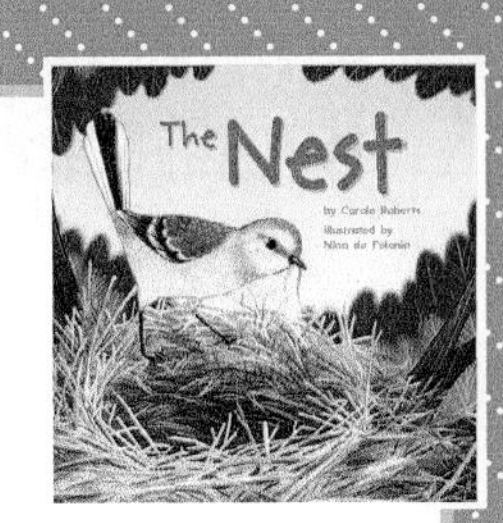

Use details from **The Nest** to answer these questions with a partner.

1. **Ask and Answer Questions** What questions did you ask yourself before, during, and after reading? How did they help you understand **The Nest**?

2. What important things happen after the bird lays the eggs?

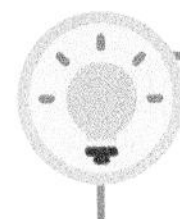

Talking Tip

Be polite. Wait for your turn to tell your idea to your partner.

I think that ____________.

31

Academic Discussion

Use the TURN AND TALK routine. Remind children to follow agreed-upon rules for discussion, such as being polite, listening carefully, and waiting for your turn to talk.

Possible responses:

1. *Accept reasonable responses.* DOK 2
2. *The bird sits on the eggs to keep them warm. The eggs hatch. The mom and dad birds feed the babies. The baby birds grow bigger and learn to fly.* DOK 2

Cite Text Evidence

READ Together

Write a Journal Entry

PROMPT Think about what the birds did in **The Nest.** Write a journal entry to show what you learned.

PLAN First, draw a picture that shows an interesting fact you learned about birds or eggs.

Write About Reading

- **Read aloud** the prompt.
- **Lead a discussion** in which children recall what the adult and baby birds did during the story. Encourage them to tell the events that happened in the story in order. Tell them to use text evidence to support their ideas.
- Then read aloud the Plan section. Have children use ideas from the discussion in their drawings. Encourage them to add details to their drawings.

DOK 3

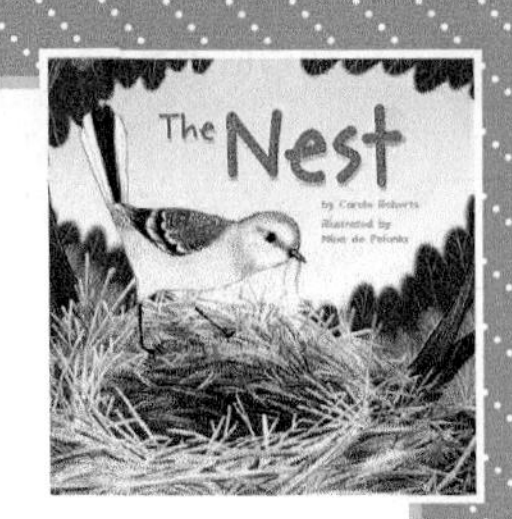

WRITE Now write today's date. Write a sentence or two to explain the information your picture shows. Remember to:

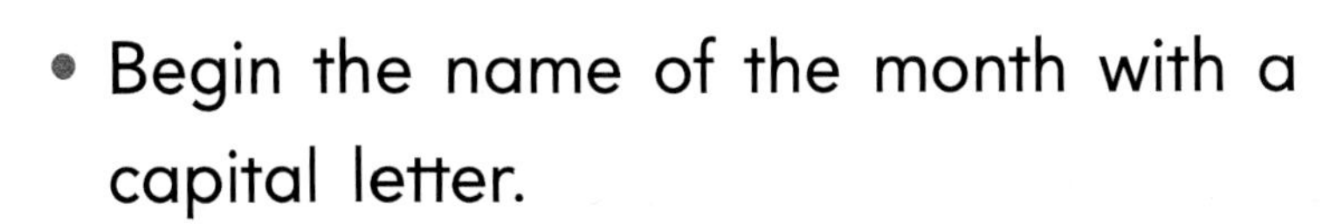

- Begin the name of the month with a capital letter.

- Be sure each sentence tells a complete idea.

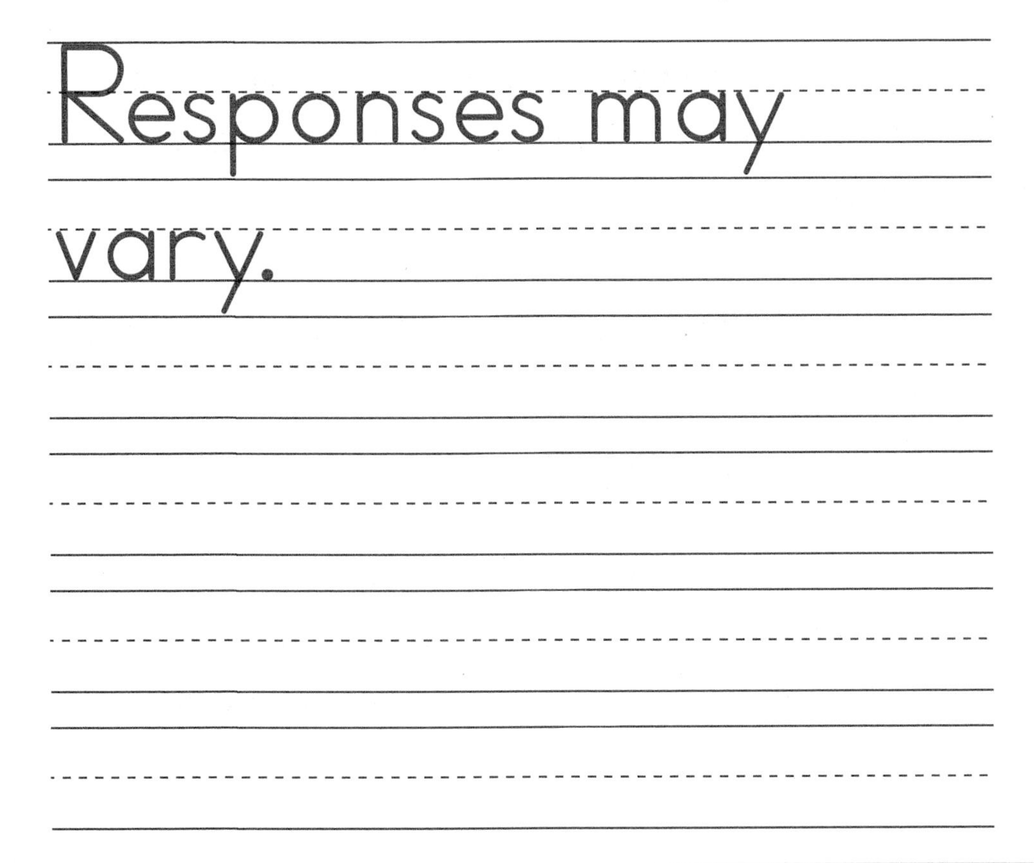

33

Write About Reading

- **Read aloud** the Write section.
- **Encourage children** to write the name of the month with a capital letter and check to make sure that their sentences describe their pictures tell a complete idea.

DOK 3

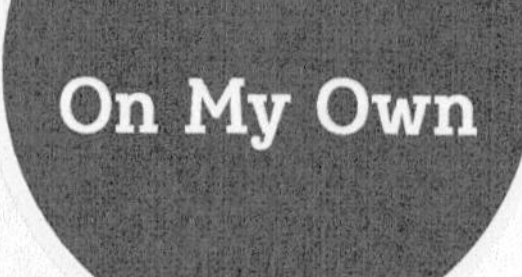

Independent Close Reading

Have children close read and annotate "The Pet Plan" on their own during small-group or independent work time. As needed, **use the Scaffolded Support notes** that follow to guide children who need additional help.

Scaffolded Support

As needed, remind children to:

- ask and answer questions before, during, and after reading to help them understand and enjoy the story.
- use details in the words and pictures, and the words *first*, *next*, and *last* to identify and describe the most important events at the beginning, middle, and end of the story.

DOK 2

Prepare to Read

GENRE STUDY **Realistic fiction** stories are made up but could happen in real life.

MAKE A PREDICTION Preview **The Pet Plan**. Think about events that could really happen in this realistic fiction story. What do you think it will be about?

The pet will get out of its home.

SET A PURPOSE Ask yourself questions before, during, and after you read to help you understand what the kids do when something happens to the pet.

The Pet Plan

READ Describe an important event that happens in the beginning.

The kids had a pet at school.
They fed the pet every day.
But one day, the pet got out!
"Will we find our pet?" asked Jen.
"Yes!" said Ned. "I have a plan."

Close Reading Tip
Number the main events in order.

CHECK MY UNDERSTANDING

Write a question you have about the story. Then read on to see if you can find the answer.

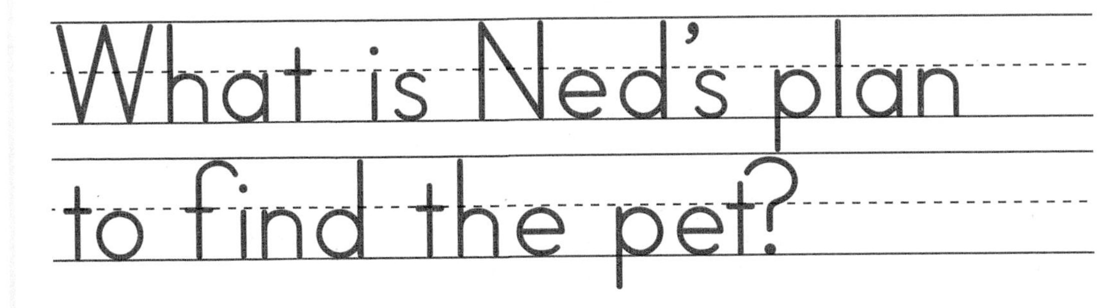

Scaffolded Support

As needed, guide children to:

- ask questions that begin with *who, what, where, when, why,* or *how.*
- use the words *first, next,* and *last* to describe story events.

DOK 2

READ Use details in the words and picture to describe important events that happen next. Underline words that help show the order of events.

"First, look in every place in the room," said Ned.
They did not find the pet.
"Then we will put out cookies," said Ned.
The kids sat and sat.
Zip! Zip! The pet ran out to get a cookie.
"Get the pet!" said Jim.
At last, the kids got the pet!
Then it was safe and warm in its nest.

Close Reading Tip

Put a ? by the parts you have questions about.

Scaffolded Support

As needed, remind children that:

- asking and answering questions as they read will help them make sure they understand what is happening in the story.
- they can use details in the words and illustrations to help them answer their questions.
- identifying and using words that name sequences, such as *first*, *next*, and *last*, will help them understand and tell about the order of story events.

DOK 2

CHECK MY UNDERSTANDING

Describe what happens to the pet at the end of the story.

The kids get the pet. They put it back into its home. It is safe.

Cite Text Evidence

WRITE ABOUT IT What do you think happens next in the story? Add on to the story. Use words like **first, next, then,** and **last** to tell the events in order.

The next day, the pet got out again! First, it ran outside. The kids ran after it. Then they found the pet asleep in an old bird's nest!

Scaffolded Support

As needed, guide children to think about the last important event in the story. Encourage them to ask themselves questions, such as: *What did the kids do the next day? What happens to the pet?* Remind them to use sequence words to tell the events in order.

DOK 2

READ FOR UNDERSTANDING

Introduce the Text

- **Read aloud** and discuss the information about the genre.
- **Guide children** to set a purpose for reading to practice creating mental images.
- **Provide information** about the author, James Bruchac.
- Tell children to look for and think about the Power Words as they read.

Guided Practice

Prepare to Read

GENRE STUDY **Folktales** are stories from long ago that have been told over and over. Look for:

- animals that act and talk like people
- storytelling phrases like **long ago**
- the reason an author tells a story

POWER WORDS
dull
thank
once

SET A PURPOSE Make pictures in your mind as you read. Words that tell how things look, sound, feel, taste, or smell and words about feelings can help you **create mental images**.

Meet James Bruchac.

38

Blue Bird and Coyote

a Native American tale, as told by James Bruchac
illustrated by Chris Lensch

 READ FOR UNDERSTANDING

Make Predictions

- **Page through** the beginning of *Blue Bird and Coyote* with children.
- Have them **use prior knowledge** and what they know about folktales to predict what the story will be about. Tell children they will **return to their predictions** after they finish reading the story.

DOK 2

 READ FOR UNDERSTANDING

Concept Words

As children read *Blue Bird and Coyote*, they may see familiar words from their speaking and listening vocabularies that they may not know how to read yet. Write these words on the board, read them aloud, and discuss their meanings as needed.

- blue
- color
- dusty
- gray
- green

READ FOR UNDERSTANDING

ASK: What does Blue Bird look like? *(She is a gray and dull bird.)*

FOLLOW-UP: How do you know? *(The words say she is gray and dull; the picture shows a bird with gray feathers.)*

ANNOTATION TIP: Have children underline the words that describe Blue Bird.

DOK 2

READ FOR UNDERSTANDING

Quick Teach Words As needed to support comprehension, briefly explain the meaning of *long ago* in this context.

- The phrase *long ago* means that something happened at a time in the past. Explain that folktales often begin with this phrase to show that the story happened many years ago.

Long ago, Blue Bird was not blue.
She was gray and dull.
How did she get her color?

40

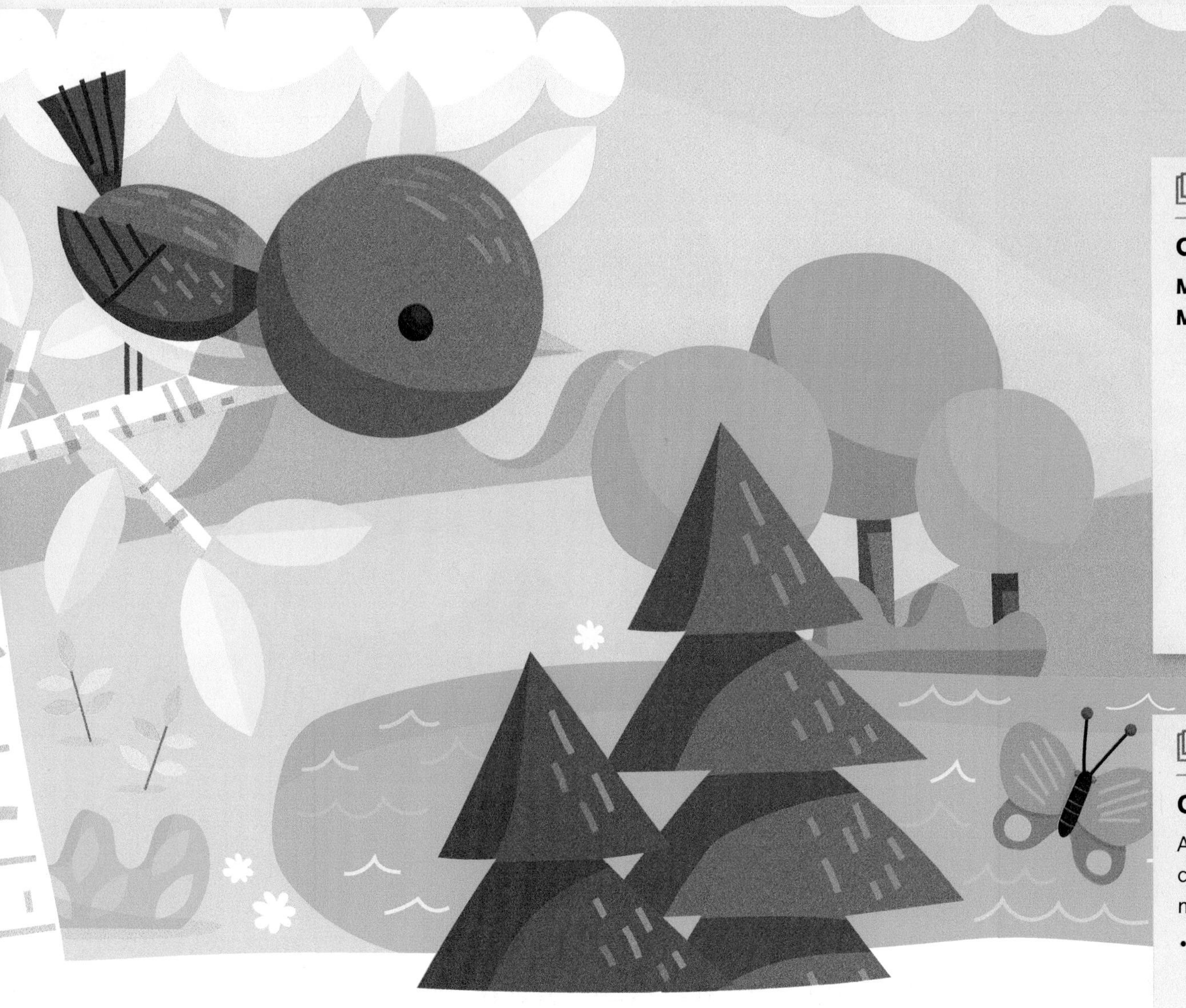

One day, Gray Bird saw a lake.
It was beautiful!
A blue butterfly was at the lake.

41

READ FOR UNDERSTANDING

Create Mental Images

MODEL CREATING A MENTAL IMAGE

THINK ALOUD *The text says that Gray Bird saw a beautiful lake and a blue butterfly. The illustration shows Gray Bird perched on a branch over the lake. I picture a brightly colored butterfly and lake. I also picture that the lake is a very quiet and peaceful place.*

DOK 2

READ FOR UNDERSTANDING

Quick Teach Words

As needed to support comprehension, briefly explain the meaning of *lake* in this context.

- A *lake* is a large body of water that is surrounded by land.

READ FOR UNDERSTANDING

ASK: Why do you think Gray Bird asks Butterfly how she got her color? *(Possible responses: She thinks the butterfly's color is beautiful; she wants to be that color, too.)*

DOK 2

"How did you get your color?"
asked Gray Bird.
"It is from the lake," said Butterfly.

42

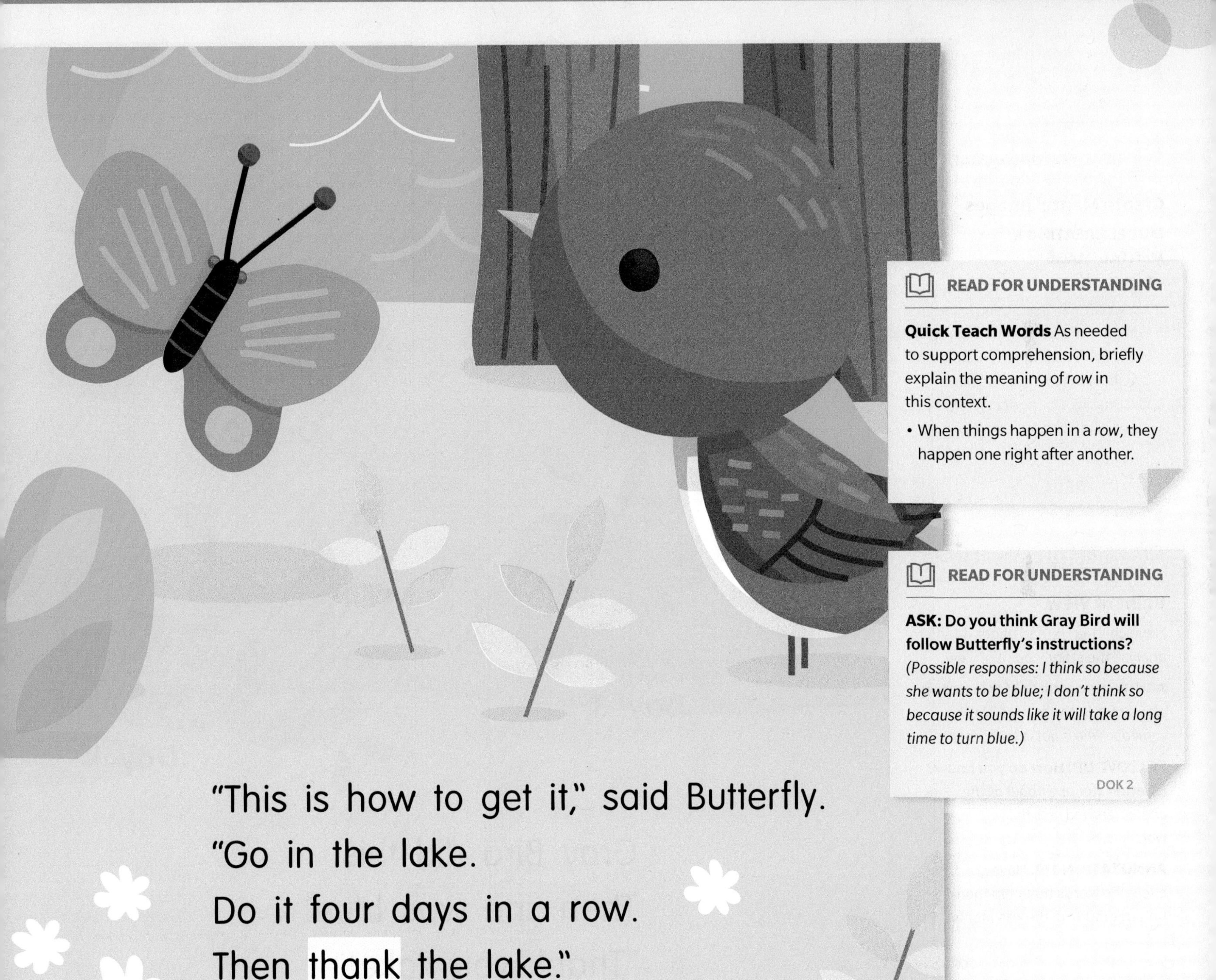

"This is how to get it," said Butterfly.
"Go in the lake.
Do it four days in a row.
Then thank the lake."

43

READ FOR UNDERSTANDING

Quick Teach Words As needed to support comprehension, briefly explain the meaning of *row* in this context.

- When things happen in a *row*, they happen one right after another.

READ FOR UNDERSTANDING

ASK: Do you think Gray Bird will follow Butterfly's instructions? *(Possible responses: I think so because she wants to be blue; I don't think so because it sounds like it will take a long time to turn blue.)*

DOK 2

READ FOR UNDERSTANDING

Create Mental Images

MODEL CREATING A MENTAL IMAGE

THINK ALOUD *The illustration shows Gray Bird splashing in the lake. I imagine the splashing sounds she makes. The text says she is blue and I see she is a different color in the illustrations. I picture her feathers slowly changing from gray to blue.*

DOK 2

TARGETED CLOSE READ

Point of View

Have children reread pages 44–45 to analyze the story's point of view.

ASK: Is the narrator of this story a character in the story? *(No, it is someone who is not in the story.)*

FOLLOW-UP: How do you know? *(The narrator tells about all the characters and uses the word she.)*

ANNOTATION TIP: Have children circle the words that help them understand who the narrator is.

DOK 3

Gray Bird did this.
Then she was blue!
"Thank you, lake!"

44

Long ago, Coyote was green.
Coyote saw Blue Bird.
"How did you get your color?" asked Coyote.
"I will tell you," said Blue Bird.
And she did.

45

READ FOR UNDERSTANDING

Quick Teach Words

As needed to support comprehension, briefly explain the meaning of *Coyote* in this context.

- A *coyote* is an animal that looks like a small wolf. *Coyotes* are often characters in folktales.

ANNOTATION TIP: Have children circle the uppercase *C* in the word *Coyote*. Point out that *Coyote* is the name of a character in this story.

READ FOR UNDERSTANDING

Phonics/Decoding in Context

Have children point to the words *will* and *tell*. Remind them that double consonants at the end of a word stand for the same sound. Review that when there is only one vowel in a word and it is followed by two of the same consonants, it usually stands for its short vowel sound. **Model blending** the sounds in each word: /w/ /ĭ/ /l/, *will;* /t/ /ĕ/ /l/, *tell*. Have children repeat.

READ FOR UNDERSTANDING

Create Mental Images

ASK: What picture do you make in your mind about Coyote? *(Possible response: I picture Coyote jumping in and out of the lake and turning more blue after each jump. I imagine big splashing sounds.)*

READ FOR UNDERSTANDING

Phonics/Decoding in Context

Have children point to the word all. Remind them that double consonants at the end of a word stand for the same sound. **Model blending** the sounds in the word: /ŏ/ /l/, *all*. Have children repeat.

Coyote went in the lake.
But, he did all four dips in one day!
Once he was blue, Coyote got out.
He did not thank the lake.

Coyote ran off to tell his friends.
But Coyote fell!
He went down,
down,
down a big hill.

47

Notice & Note

Again and Again

- **Remind children** that if they see a word or picture that is repeated in a story, they should stop to notice and note. Explain that this can help them understand the story better or create a mental image about something important that is happening in the story.
- **Have children explain** why they might use this strategy on page 47. *(Coyote fell down a hill. The author says he fell down, down, down.)*

ANNOTATION TIP: Have children circle the word that repeats.

- **Remind them** of the Anchor Question: **Why might the author repeat this word again and again?** *(The author wants to show that Coyote fell a long distance. These repeated words help me picture him tumbling down a long, steep hill.)*

DOK 2

Coyote got up.
Now he was all dusty and dull!

To this day, Blue Bird is blue.
And Coyote is dusty gray.

48

TARGETED CLOSE READ

Point of View

Have children reread page 48 to analyze the story's point of view.

ASK: From which point of view is this story told? *(third-person)*

FOLLOW-UP: How do you know? *(The narrator tells about all the characters and uses the word* he.*)*

ANNOTATION TIP: Have children circle the words that help them understand which point of view the story is told from.

DOK 3

READ FOR UNDERSTANDING

Wrap Up

Revisit the predictions children made before reading. Have them confirm or correct their predictions using evidence from the text and pictures.

DOK 2

Respond to Reading

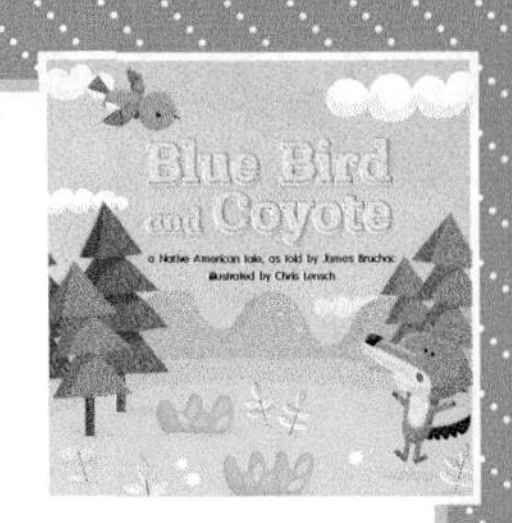

Use details from **Blue Bird and Coyote** to answer these questions with a partner.

1. **Create Mental Images** What pictures did you make in your mind when Blue Bird and Coyote got their colors? What words helped you create those pictures?

2. What do you think the author wants you to learn from the story?

Listening Tip

Listen carefully. Think about the meaning of what your partner is saying.

Academic Discussion

Use the TURN AND TALK routine. Remind children to follow agreed-upon rules for discussion, such as listening carefully and building on others' ideas.

Possible responses:

1. *Accept reasonable responses.* DOK 2
2. *When you want something badly, it is best to follow directions and be patient.* DOK 2

Cite Text Evidence

READ Together

Write a Story Ending

PROMPT Coyote still wants blue fur! How will he get it? Make up an ending to add to **Blue Bird and Coyote**.

PLAN What is Coyote's new plan to get blue fur? Add three ideas to the chart.

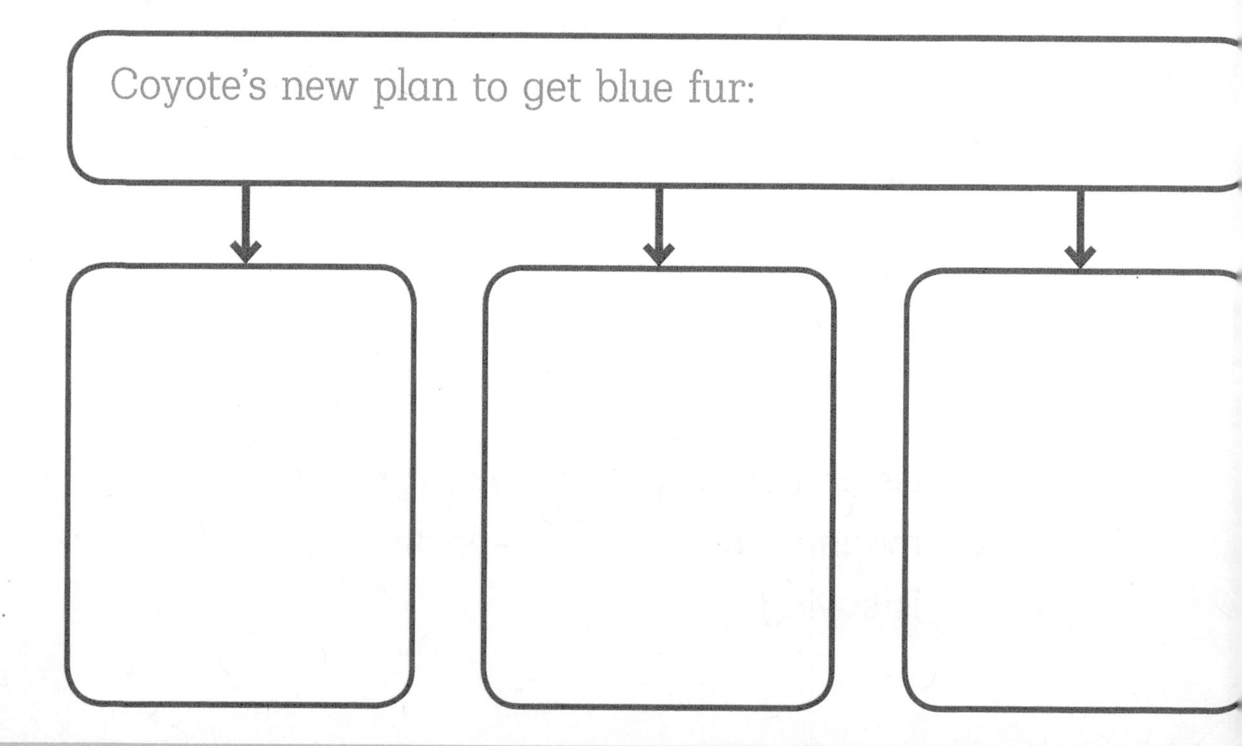

Write About Reading

- **Read aloud** the prompt.
- **Lead a discussion** in which children share what they know about Coyote and what he might do to get blue fur.
- Then read aloud the Plan section. Have children use ideas from the discussion in their charts.

DOK 3

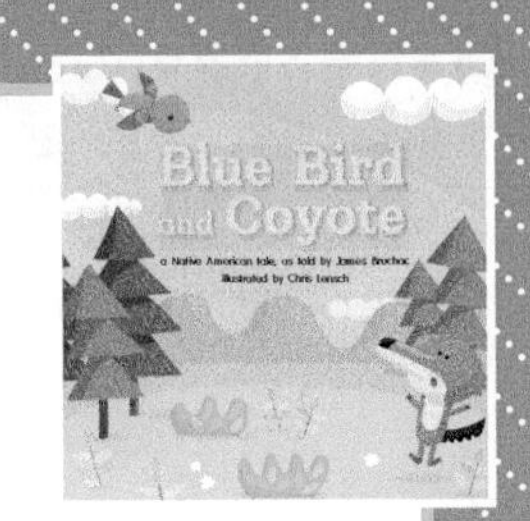

WRITE Now write what happens next in the story. Use another sheet of paper if you need to. Remember to:

- Tell how Coyote solves his problem.
- Be sure each sentence tells a complete idea.

Responses may vary.

Write About Reading

- **Read aloud** the Write section.
- **Encourage children** to focus on one idea about how Coyote resolves his problem. Have them tell what he does and what happens in sentences that tell a complete idea.

DOK 3

Independent Close Reading

Have children close read and annotate "The Nut" on their own during small-group or independent work time. As needed, **use the Scaffolded Support notes** that follow to guide children who need additional help.

Scaffolded Support

As needed, guide children to:

- create mental images about the characters and what is happening. Have them identify details in the text, including descriptive language, that helped them create those images.
- look for clues that will help them identify from whose point of view the story is told and whether its narrator is a character in the story or not.

DOK 3

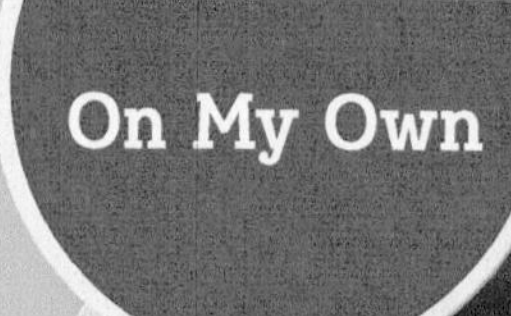

Prepare to Read

GENRE STUDY **Folktales** are stories from long ago that have been told over and over.

MAKE A PREDICTION Preview **The Nut**. Blue Bird and Coyote are together again! This time they find a nut. What do you think will happen?

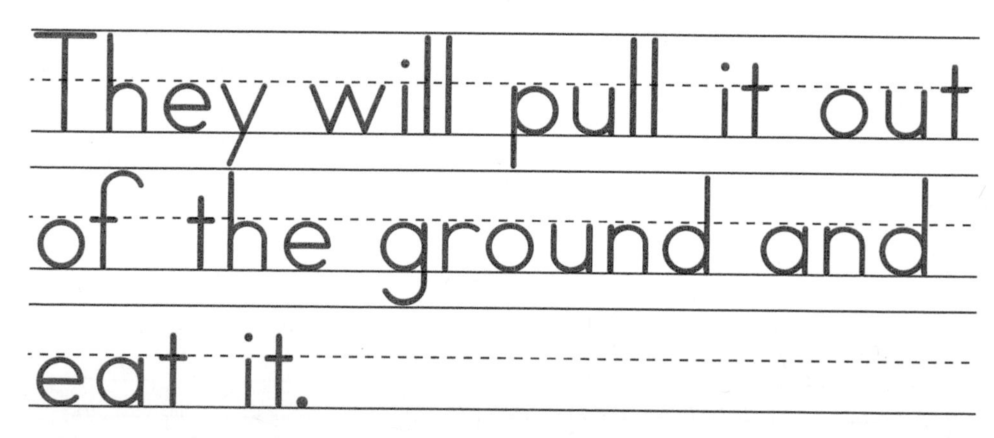

SET A PURPOSE Read to find out what Blue Bird and Coyote do with the nut. Find out if your prediction is right.

52

The Nut

READ Underline words that help you imagine what the nut is like.

One day, Blue Bird and Coyote find a
BIG green nut. Yum!
They tug, but the nut will not pop out!
Fox runs up and sees the big green nut.
Yum! Fox will help. ▶

Close Reading Tip
Write C when you make a connection.

CHECK MY UNDERSTANDING

Picture in your mind what the nut is like. Why won't it come out of the ground?

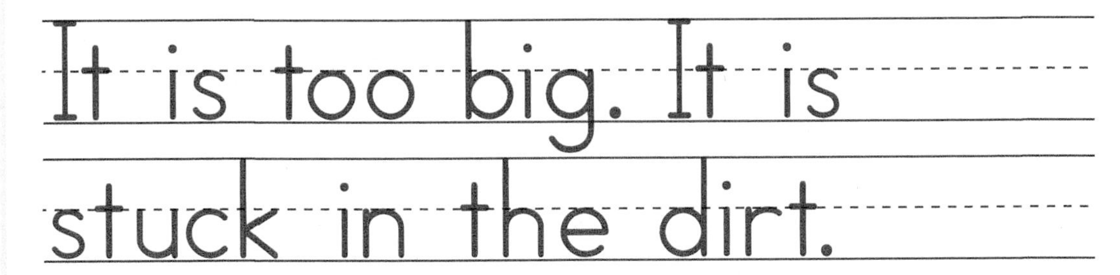

53

Scaffolded Support

As needed, remind children to:

- use details in the text and illustrations to help them make a mental image of the nut.
- make connections by looking for ways one part of the text is like or unlike another part of the text , a different text, an experience they had, or something in society.

DOK 2

READ Does one of the characters tell this story or is it a person not in the story? Underline words that tell you.

Cat and Dog help, too.
They all tug and tug and tug.
But the nut will not pop out!
Then Bug said that she will help.
"How can you help?" asked Fox.
"I have lots of little legs," she said.
They all tug together and . . .
POP! The big nut is out!
"Thank you, friends!" said Coyote.

Close Reading Tip
Put a ! by a surprising part.

Scaffolded Support

As needed, remind children that:

- when the narrator is not a character in the story, the narrator uses words such as *he, she,* and *they.*
- when the narrator is a character in the story, the narrator uses words like *I, me,* and *we.*
- something that is surprising is something that is not expected to happen.

DOK 2

CHECK MY UNDERSTANDING

What might the characters do with the nut? Why?

They will eat the nut together. They all helped get it out.

Cite Text Evidence

WRITE ABOUT IT Think about what Coyote is like in **Blue Bird and Coyote** and **The Nut.** How are the things he does different in both stories? Why do you think he does different things?

In Blue Bird and Coyote, Coyote acts silly. He doesn't thank the lake. In The Nut, he is nicer. He has learned to say thank you.

55

Scaffolded Support

As needed, guide children to think about what the characters say and do in each story, and how their words and actions are alike and different.

DOK 3

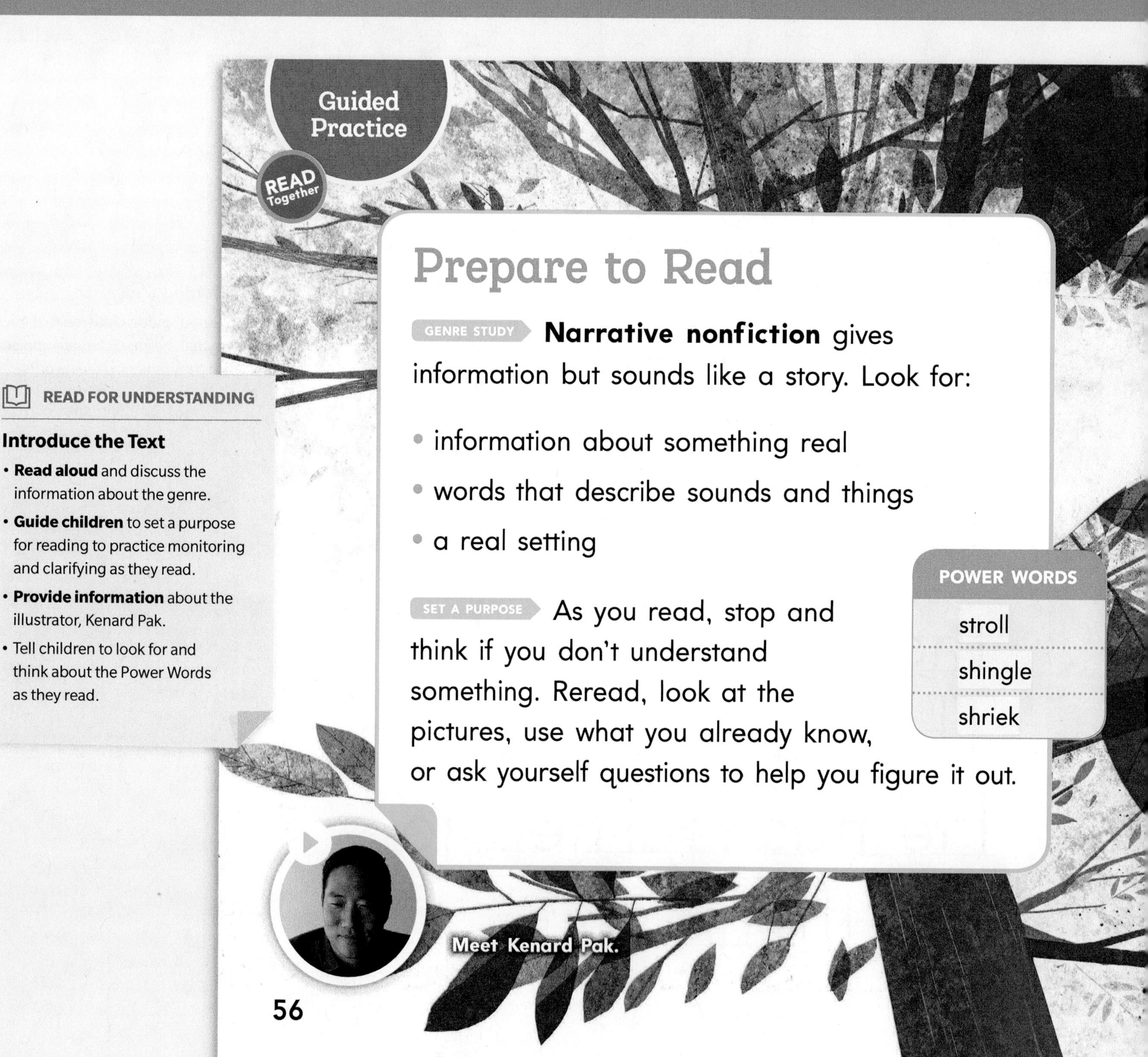

Guided Practice

READ Together

Prepare to Read

GENRE STUDY **Narrative nonfiction** gives information but sounds like a story. Look for:

- information about something real
- words that describe sounds and things
- a real setting

SET A PURPOSE As you read, stop and think if you don't understand something. Reread, look at the pictures, use what you already know, or ask yourself questions to help you figure it out.

POWER WORDS
stroll
shingle
shriek

Meet Kenard Pak.

56

READ FOR UNDERSTANDING

Introduce the Text

- **Read aloud** and discuss the information about the genre.
- **Guide children** to set a purpose for reading to practice monitoring and clarifying as they read.
- **Provide information** about the illustrator, Kenard Pak.
- Tell children to look for and think about the Power Words as they read.

READ FOR UNDERSTANDING

Make Predictions

- **Page through** the beginning of *Have You Heard the Nesting Bird?* with children.
- Have them **use prior knowledge** and the illustrations to predict what the selection will be about. Tell children they will **return to their predictions** after they finish reading the selection.

DOK 2

READ FOR UNDERSTANDING

Concept Words

As children read *Have You Heard the Nesting Bird?* they may see familiar words from their speaking and listening vocabularies that they may not know how to read yet. Write these words on the board, read them aloud, and discuss their meanings as needed.

- blue jay
- cardinal
- crow
- doves
- robin
- sparrow
- woodpecker

58

Mourning doves take their morning stroll.

coah, cooo, cooo, coooo

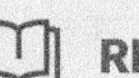

Woodpecker calls from a tree with a hole.

cuk-cuk-cuk-cuk-cuk

Starling sings from a metal pole.

whistle-ee-wee-tree

READ FOR UNDERSTANDING

Monitor and Clarify

MODEL MONITORING AND CLARIFYING

THINK ALOUD *As I read, I pause when I don't understand something. The text tells about different birds and what they are doing. It says a woodpecker calls from a tree with a hole. I can try different things to help me understand this sentence, like asking questions, rereading the text, looking for clues in the pictures, and thinking about what I already know.*

DOK 2

But have you heard the nesting bird?
"What bird? Where?"
"That robin, nesting up there."

61

READ FOR UNDERSTANDING

ASK: Who is talking on this page? *(A boy and a girl.)*

FOLLOW-UP: How do you know? *(The text shows the words in quotation marks; the picture shows a boy and girl looking up at the bird.)*

DOK 2

READ FOR UNDERSTANDING

Quick Teach Words

As needed to support comprehension, briefly explain the meaning of *heard* in this context.

- If you *heard* something, you became aware of a sound.

TARGETED CLOSE READ

Text Organization

Have children reread pages 62–63 to analyze how the author organizes the text.

ASK: How does the author organize the information? *(She describes a bird on each page.)*

FOLLOW-UP: Why do you think she does this? *(Possible response: to show how the birds are the same and different)*

ANNOTATION TIP: Have children underline the sound words that describe what kind of sound each bird makes.

DOK 3

READ FOR UNDERSTANDING

Quick Teach Words

As needed to support comprehension, briefly explain the meaning of *jingle* in this context.

- A *jingle* is a light, ringing sound.

Sparrow makes a simple jingle.

chiddik, chiddik

Swallow slides from under a shingle.

ha-ha-chit-chit-chit,
ha-ha-twitter-twit!

READ FOR UNDERSTANDING

Monitor and Clarify

ASK: Is there something on this page you do not understand? *(Possible responses: what the swallow is doing; what shingle means)*

FOLLOW-UP: What could you do to help you understand what is happening on this page? *(Possible responses: I can reread the words, I can look at the picture, I can think about what I already know about birds and what I have already learned from reading this text, and I can ask myself questions.)*

DOK 2

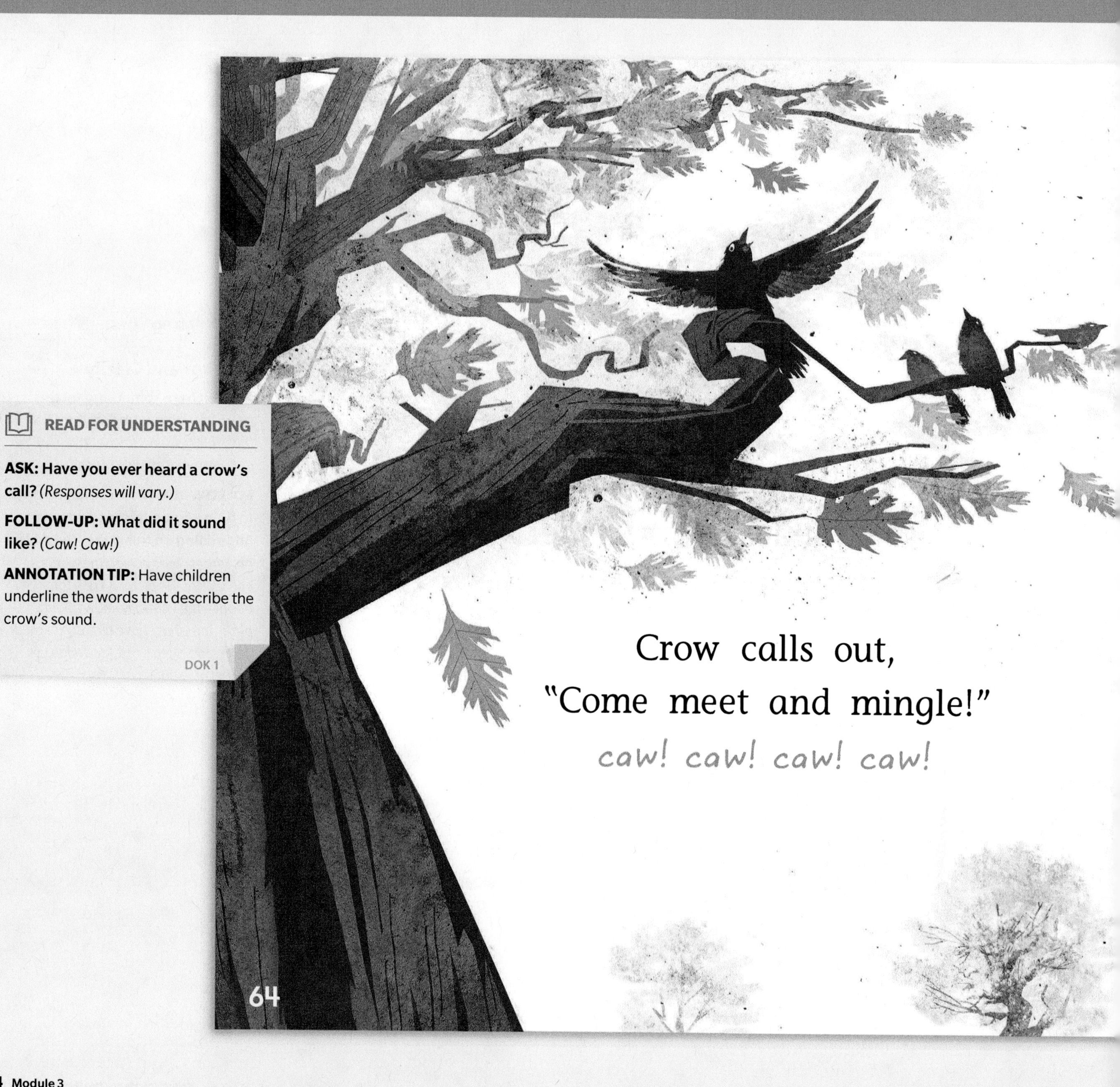

Crow calls out,
"Come meet and mingle!"
caw! caw! caw! caw!

64

READ FOR UNDERSTANDING

ASK: Have you ever heard a crow's call? *(Responses will vary.)*

FOLLOW-UP: What did it sound like? *(Caw! Caw!)*

ANNOTATION TIP: Have children underline the words that describe the crow's sound.

DOK 1

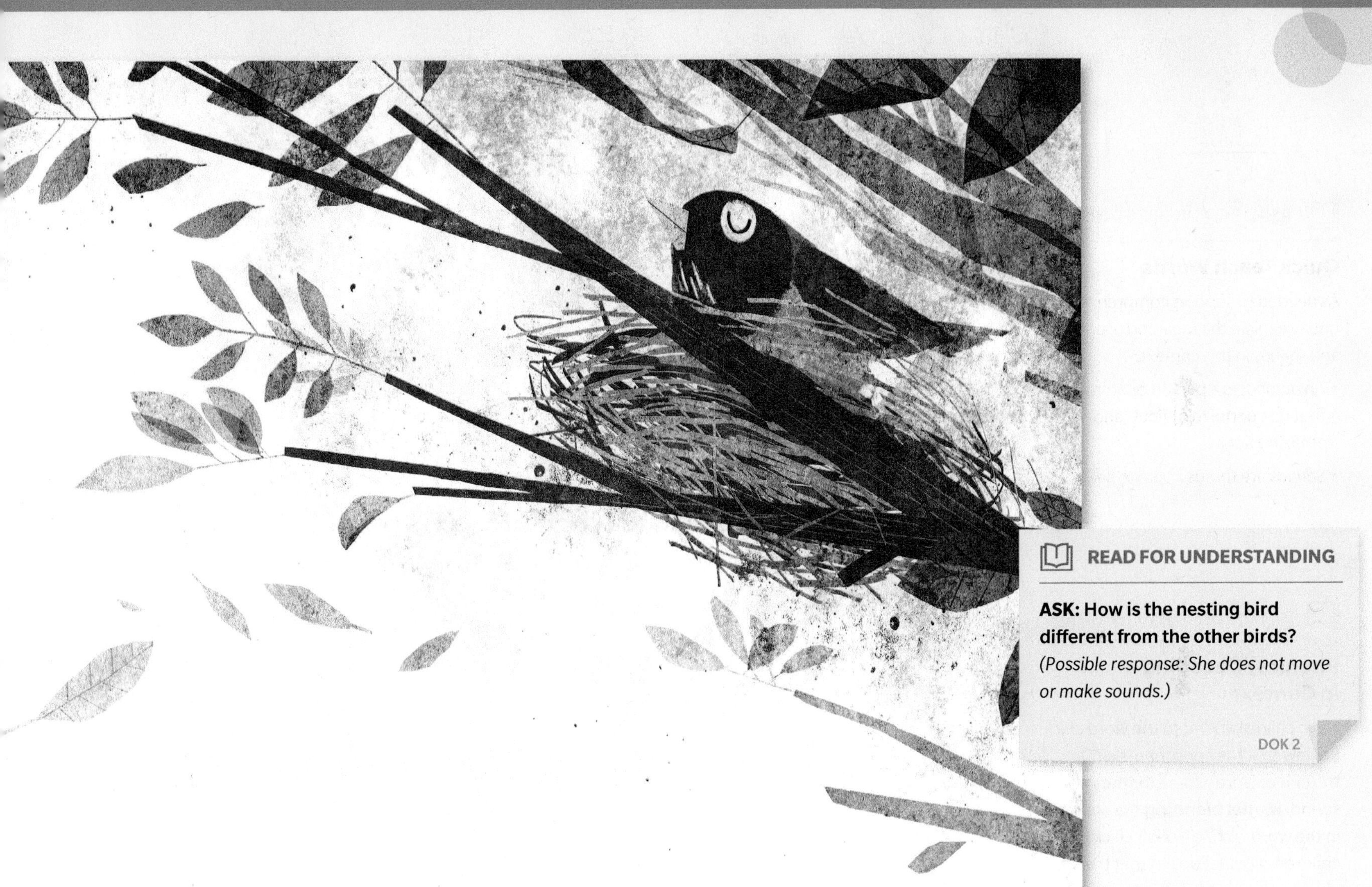

But have you heard the nesting bird?
"Not a single tweet or trill."
"This nesting bird is so still!"

65

READ FOR UNDERSTANDING

ASK: **How is the nesting bird different from the other birds?** *(Possible response: She does not move or make sounds.)*

DOK 2

READ FOR UNDERSTANDING

Quick Teach Words

As needed to support comprehension, briefly explain the meaning of *acrobat* and *sounds* in this context.

- An *acrobat* is a person or animal that can perform difficult and amazing acts.
- *Sounds* are things you can hear.

READ FOR UNDERSTANDING

Phonics/Decoding in Context

Have children point to the word *chick*. Review that the consonants *ck* at the end of words stand for the /k/ sound. **Model blending** the sounds in the word: /ch/ /ĭ/ /k/, *chick*. Have children repeat. Explain that the word *chick* is used to describe the sound the chickadee makes.

ANNOTATION TIP: Have children circle the words that describe each bird's sound.

cheer-cheer-cheer-
purdy-purdy-purdy

chick-a-dee-dee-dee

meow! meow!

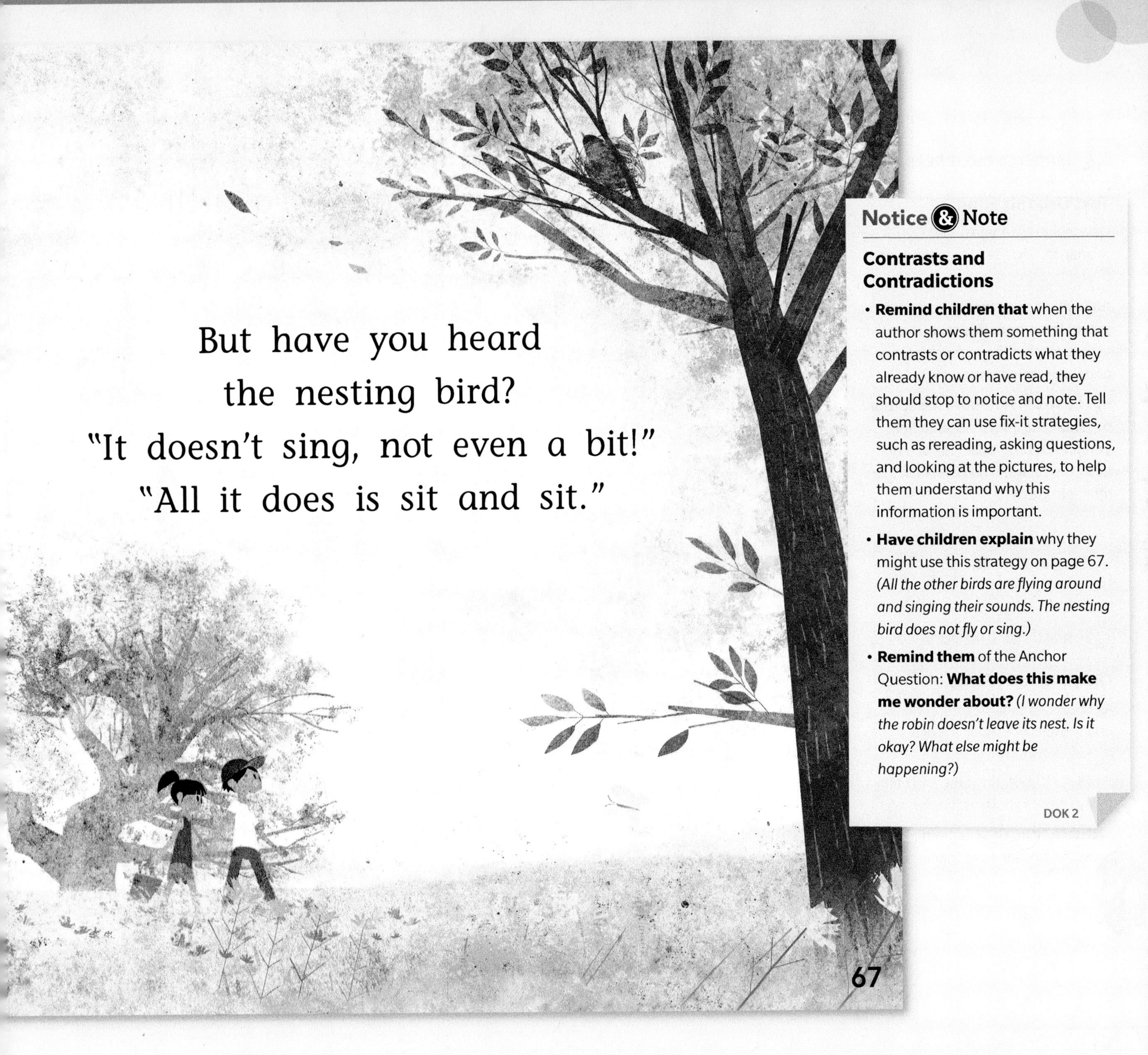

Notice & Note

Contrasts and Contradictions

- **Remind children that** when the author shows them something that contrasts or contradicts what they already know or have read, they should stop to notice and note. Tell them they can use fix-it strategies, such as rereading, asking questions, and looking at the pictures, to help them understand why this information is important.
- **Have children explain** why they might use this strategy on page 67. *(All the other birds are flying around and singing their sounds. The nesting bird does not fly or sing.)*
- **Remind them** of the Anchor Question: **What does this make me wonder about?** *(I wonder why the robin doesn't leave its nest. Is it okay? What else might be happening?)*

DOK 2

TARGETED CLOSE READ

Text Organization

Have children reread pages 68–69 to analyze how the author organizes the text.

ASK: What does the author want you to learn from this text? *(that the nesting bird is different from the other birds because it does not sing)*

FOLLOW-UP: How does the author organize the information to help you understand this? *(The author describes each bird and its sound, one after the other.)*

DOK 3

READ FOR UNDERSTANDING

Quick Teach Words

As needed to support comprehension, briefly explain the meaning of *twilight* in this context.

- *Twilight* is the light at the end of the day when night is just beginning.

ANNOTATION TIP: Guide children to circle the smaller word *light* in *twilight*.

Blue jay's shriek is
as sharp as a drill.

jay! jay! jay! jay!

Whip-poor-will has
his favorite trill.

whip-poor-will whip-poor-will

Wood thrush turns
the twilight still.

ee-oh-lay ee-oh-laaay

68

But have you heard the nesting bird?
"It hasn't sung a single song."
"This bird has been sitting for so long!"

69

READ FOR UNDERSTANDING

ANNOTATION TIP: Ask children to underline the words that describe what the robin has been doing throughout the story.

ASK: Why do you think the children keep wondering about the nesting bird? *(Possible responses: The author wants us to wonder too; the author wants to remind us of what the nesting bird does now because it will probably do something different at the end of the story.)*

DOK 3

READ FOR UNDERSTANDING

ASK: What is the nesting bird doing? *(She looks like she is about to fly.)*

FOLLOW-UP: How do you know? *(Possible responses: She is standing on the nest and her wings are open; I know that birds open their wings when they are going to fly.)*

DOK 2

Wait, what's that . . . ?

Tapping *Cracking*

"Something made a little sound!"

Breaking *Shaking*

"The bird is starting to move around!"

Ruffling *Shuffling*

READ FOR UNDERSTANDING

Monitor and Clarify

MODEL MONITORING AND CLARIFYING

THINK ALOUD *The sound words on this page are different from the ones on the previous pages. What can I do to make sure I understand? I can ask myself a question, think about what I know, look at the picture, and reread. I ask myself, "Do those words describe the sounds a robin makes?" I'll reread the page. Now I see! Those words describe the sounds coming from the robin's nest, not the sounds a robin makes.*

DOK 2

72

"The bird flew off with something blue."

Cheeping Peeping

"Look! Another robin is coming too!"

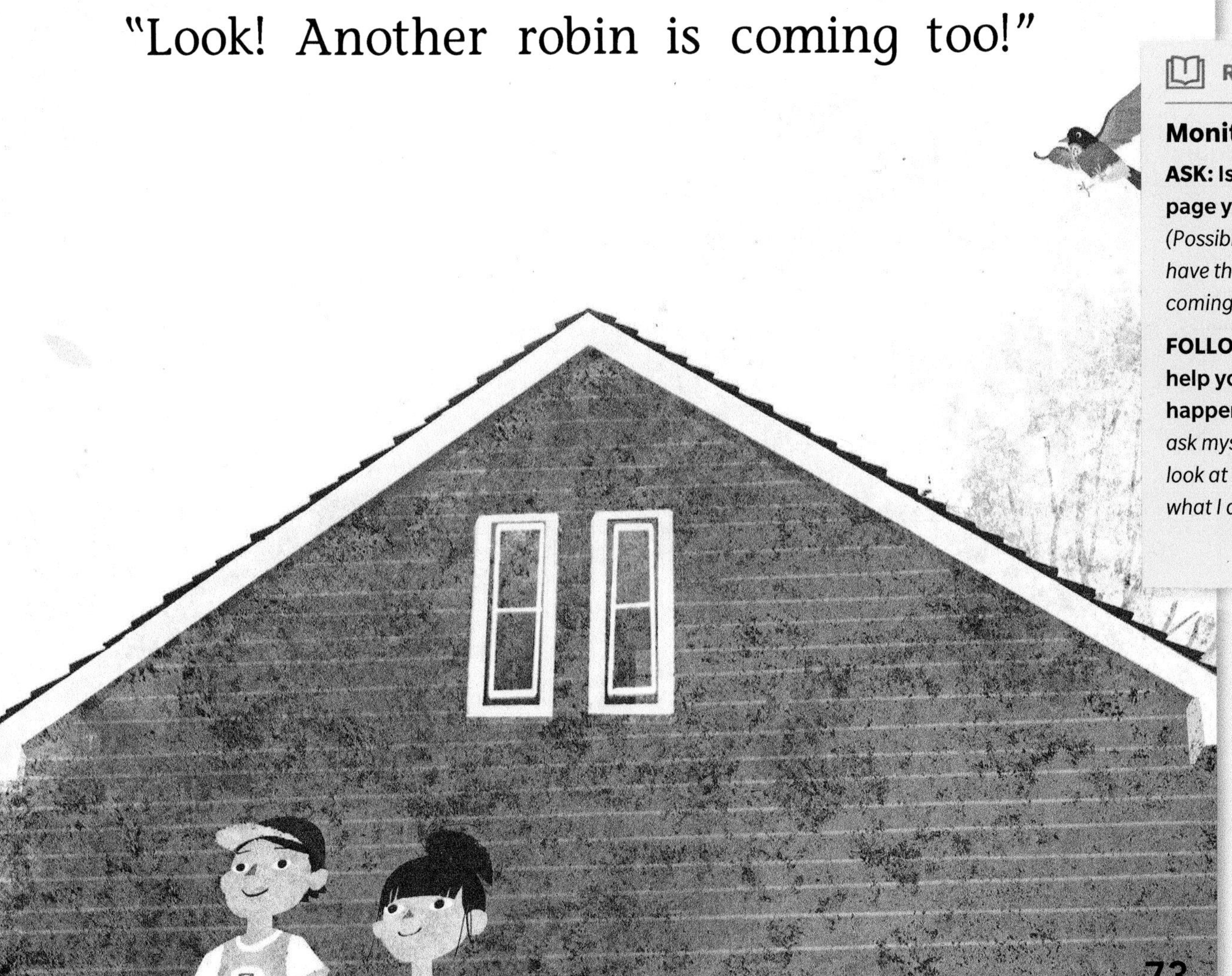

73

READ FOR UNDERSTANDING

Monitor and Clarify

ASK: Is there something on this page you do not understand? *(Possible responses: What does the bird have that is blue? Why is another bird coming to the nest?)*

FOLLOW-UP: What could you do to help you understand what is happening? *(Possible responses: I can ask myself questions, keep reading, look at the pictures, and think about what I already know.)*

DOK 2

READ FOR UNDERSTANDING

Wrap Up

Revisit the predictions children made before reading. Have them confirm or correct their predictions using evidence from the text and pictures.

DOK 2

Respond to Reading

READ Together

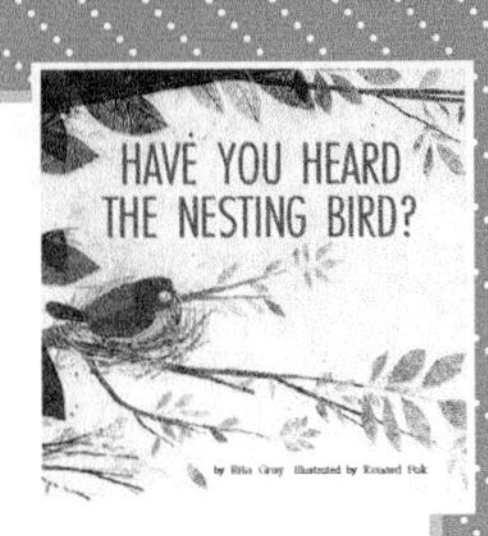

Use details from **Have You Heard the Nesting Bird?** to answer these questions with a partner.

1. **Monitor and Clarify** When you came to a part of the text you did not understand, what did you do to try to figure it out?

2. Why does the nesting bird sit so long?

Talking Tip

Ask a question if you are not sure about your partner's ideas.

Why did you say ________?

75

Academic Discussion

Use the TURN AND TALK routine. Remind children to follow agreed-upon rules for discussion, such as listening carefully and asking questions if you are unsure about your partner's ideas.

Possible responses:

1. *I reread, looked carefully at the pictures, asked myself questions, and thought about what I already knew.* DOK 2
2. *She sits on the eggs to keep them warm and help them hatch.* DOK 2

Cite Text Evidence

READ Together

Write a Story

PROMPT Imagine that you are with the kids in **Have You Heard the Nesting Bird?** What do you see the nesting bird do?

PLAN Draw pictures to show the main things the nesting bird does **first, next,** and **last.**

First	Next	Last

76

Write About Reading

- **Read aloud** the prompt.
- **Lead a discussion** in which children recount the things that the kids in the text saw. Tell them to use text evidence to support their ideas.
- Then read aloud the Plan section. Have children use information from the discussion in their pictures.

DOK 3

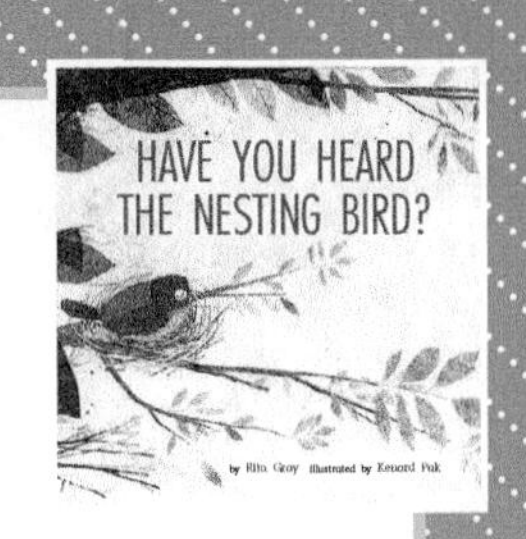

WRITE Now write your own version of the story. Tell what you saw the nesting bird do. Use another sheet of paper if you need it. Remember to:

- Use **first, next,** and **last** to show the order of events.
- Use words to describe the nesting bird.

Responses may vary.

Write About Reading

- **Read aloud** the Write section.
- **Guide children** to add details to their writing that give more information about the nesting bird and what they saw. Have them use sequence words and describing words in their writing.

DOK 3

Independent Close Reading

Have children close read and annotate "Bird News" on their own during small-group or independent work time. As needed, **use the Scaffolded Support notes** that follow to guide children who need additional help.

Scaffolded Support

As needed, remind children that:

- if something in the text does not make sense, they can reread, look at the illustrations, ask questions, and think about what they already know to help them figure it out.
- authors organize their writing to fit the topic. One type of organization is description, which means that the text describes one thing and then another.

DOK 3

Prepare to Read

GENRE STUDY **Narrative nonfiction** gives information but sounds like a story.

MAKE A PREDICTION Preview **Bird News**. A student author wrote a newspaper story about real birds. What do you think you will learn?

I will learn about interesting things different birds do.

SET A PURPOSE Read to find out which birds the student saw and what they are like. If a part is not clear, reread, look at the pictures, use what you know, or ask yourself questions to figure it out.

78

Bird News

READ What is the author describing in this part?

This is my bird news!
I saw a crow in my neighborhood.
Like all birds, crows have many feathers and a beak.
This crow had a nest made of twigs.
It had four dull-blue eggs in its nest.

Close Reading Tip

Underline the important describing words.

CHECK MY UNDERSTANDING

Describe the crow. Use details from the text and photo.

a bird with a black beak and feathers

79

Scaffolded Support

As needed, remind children that:

- keeping in mind how the author organizes a text will help them understand it.
- they can reread the text to look for details that will help them answer the question.
- describing words are words that tell how something looks, feels, tastes, sounds, or smells.

DOK 3

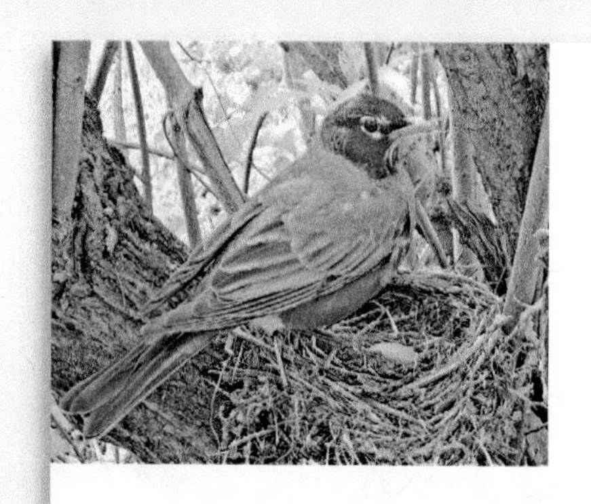

READ Underline what the author is describing in this part. The author describes two birds in two different parts. How does this help you understand the text?

I saw a mom robin, too.
It sat on a nest made of little twigs.
The mom robin got up from the nest.
I saw blue eggs with little dots.
Then I saw the robin fly back to the nest.
I will write news about the baby birds once they are out of the eggs!

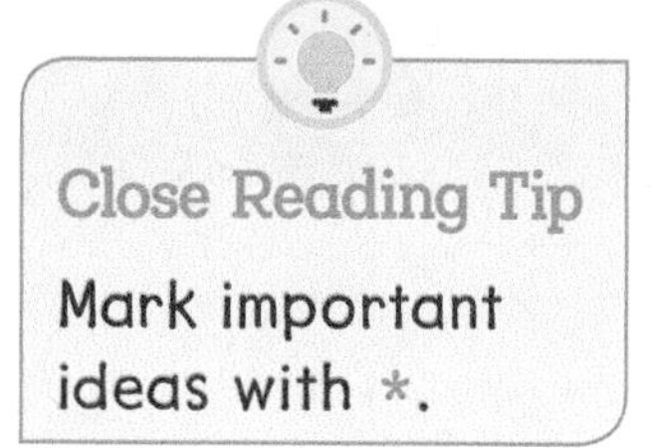

Close Reading Tip

Mark important ideas with *.

Scaffolded Support

As needed, remind children to:

- think about how the author organizes the text into different descriptions to help them understand it.
- reread the text, look at the illustrations, ask themselves questions, and think about what they already know to figure out parts they do not understand.
- think about what the author wants them to learn from the text to help them identify the important ideas.

DOK 2

CHECK MY UNDERSTANDING

When you came to a part you did not understand, what did you do to try to figure it out?

I read the sentence again and looked at the picture.

Cite Text Evidence

DRAW IT Draw a robin or a crow and its nest. Use information from **Bird News** to color and label your picture. Then share facts about the bird with a partner. Show your picture to help you describe it.

Pictures should show a robin or crow and its nest. Labels may include: robin, crow, beak, feathers, nest, eggs.

81

Scaffolded Support

As needed, guide children to reread the text to identify details to include in their pictures, labels, and descriptions.

DOK 3

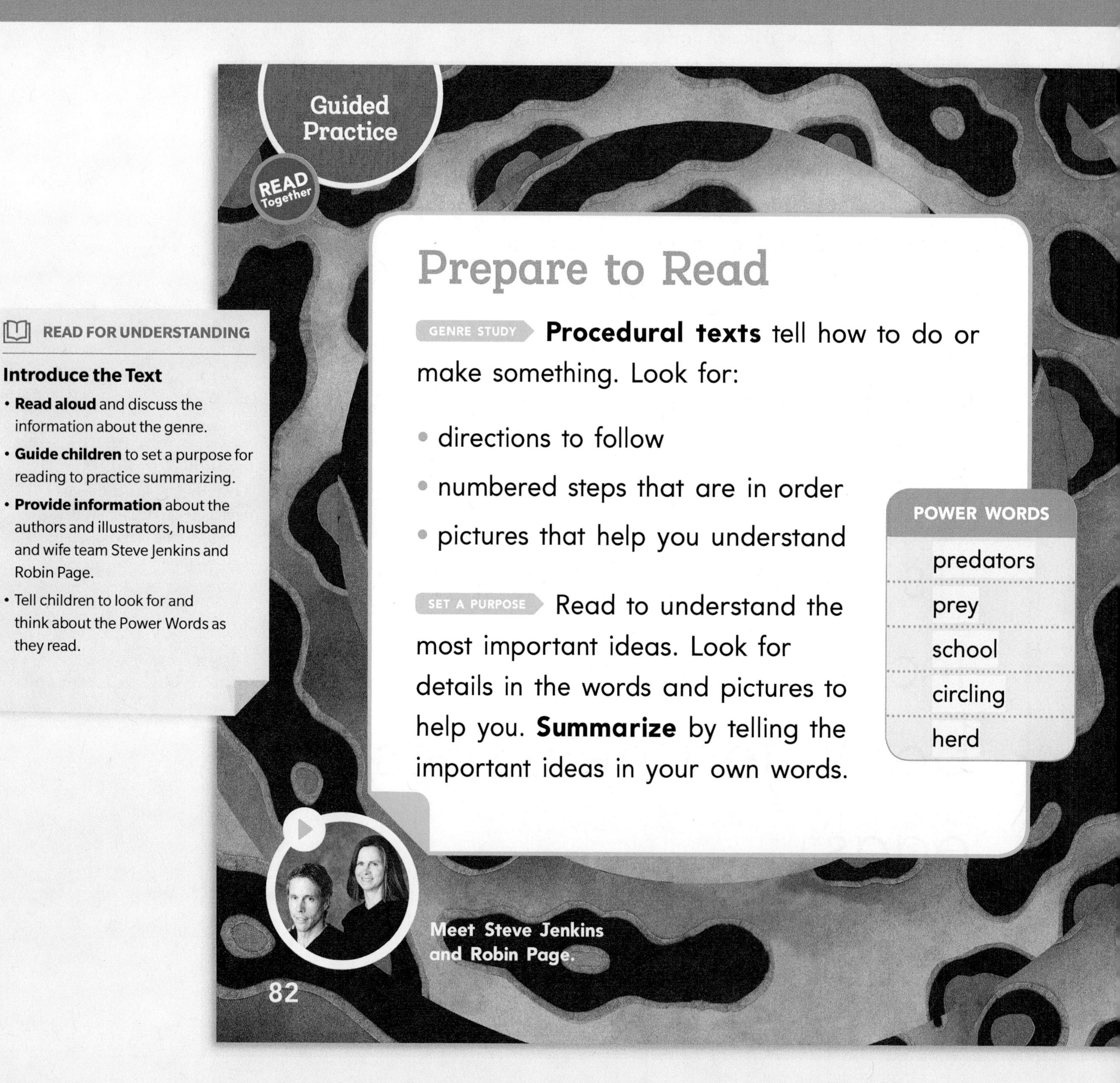

Prepare to Read

GENRE STUDY **Procedural texts** tell how to do or make something. Look for:

- directions to follow
- numbered steps that are in order
- pictures that help you understand

SET A PURPOSE Read to understand the most important ideas. Look for details in the words and pictures to help you. **Summarize** by telling the important ideas in your own words.

POWER WORDS

- predators
- prey
- school
- circling
- herd

Meet Steve Jenkins and Robin Page.

READ FOR UNDERSTANDING

Introduce the Text

- **Read aloud** and discuss the information about the genre.
- **Guide children** to set a purpose for reading to practice summarizing.
- **Provide information** about the authors and illustrators, husband and wife team Steve Jenkins and Robin Page.
- Tell children to look for and think about the Power Words as they read.

READ FOR UNDERSTANDING

Make Predictions

- **Page through** the beginning of *Step-by-Step Advice from the Animal Kingdom* with children.
- Have them **use prior knowledge** and the illustrations to predict what the text will be about. Tell children they will **return to their predictions** after they finish reading the text.

DOK 2

READ FOR UNDERSTANDING

Concept Words

As children read *Step-by-Step Advice from the Animal Kingdom,* they may see familiar words from their speaking and listening vocabularies that they may not know how to read yet. Write these words on the board, read them aloud, and discuss their meanings as needed.

- armadillo
- humpback whale
- insect
- spider

READ FOR UNDERSTANDING

Summarize

MODEL SUMMARIZING

THINK ALOUD *When I read, I want to be sure I understand the most important ideas. I ask myself, what have I learned so far? I can summarize the important details from the words and pictures in my own words to help me think about the information, and make sure I understand it. So far I have learned that an armadillo uses different parts of its body to defend itself in interesting ways.*

DOK 2

READ FOR UNDERSTANDING

ASK: **Why is freezing the first step?** *(Possible response: because it's the easiest way for the armadillo to defend itself and it works)*

FOLLOW-UP: **How do you know?** *(The text says freezing is "a good tactic".)*

ANNOTATION TIP: Circle the words that tell why it is a good idea for the armadillo to freeze.

DOK 3

How to **Defend Yourself** Like an Armadillo

1 Freeze!

Many predators don't notice prey unless it's moving. Holding still can be a good tactic.

2 Run.

Armadillos can move quickly. So can you. If freezing doesn't work, don't just sit there.

3 Dig.

Start digging a hole. Use your long claws. Work quickly! You'll soon have a burrow to hide in.

4 Swim.

You're a good swimmer. And not every predator likes to get wet.

5 Leap.

Try jumping a few feet up into the air. This can startle even the fiercest predator. It can give you time to escape.

6 Hunker down.

If all else fails, pull in your head and feet. And hope your armor persuades the attacker to give up.

85

READ FOR UNDERSTANDING

ASK: In which ways does the armadillo use its legs to defend itself? *(to run, dig, swim, and leap)*

FOLLOW-UP: Why do you think the author included the armadillo in this text? *(Possible response: because it has lots of different ways to defend itself)*

DOK 2

READ FOR UNDERSTANDING

ASK: Why is hunkering down the last step? *(Possible response: The armadillo should try to defend itself in other ways because hunkering down might not work.)*

FOLLOW-UP: How do you know? *(The text says "if all else fails" and that the armadillo should hope the attacker gives up.)*

ANNOTATION TIP: Circle the words that tell why hunkering down is the last step.

DOK 3

TARGETED CLOSE READ

Text Organization

Have children reread pages 86–89 to analyze how the author organizes the text.

ASK: How does the author explain how a spider spins a web? *(The author tells the steps in order.)*

FOLLOW-UP: What clues help you know that the text is organized in sequence? *(Each step is numbered, so that means the steps are listed in the order in which they happen.)*

ANNOTATION TIP: Have children circle the numbers in each step.

DOK 3

How to Spin a Web Like a Spider

1 Cast a line.

Cast a single silk thread into the air. If you're lucky, the breeze will catch it. It will snag on a nearby branch or other object.

2 Make a loop.

Walk across the first thread. Spin another that droops to form a U.

86

❸ Turn your U into a Y.

Drop a line from the bottom of the loose thread. Tighten it to make a Y shape.

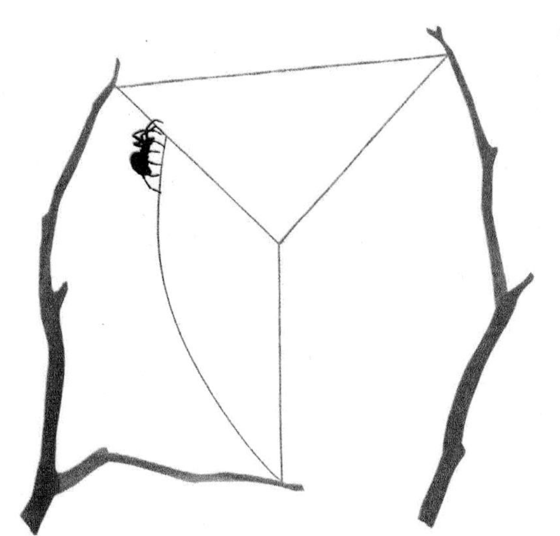

❹ Frame your web.

Spin threads that will form the borders of your web.

READ FOR UNDERSTANDING

Quick Teach Words

As needed to support comprehension, briefly explain the meaning of *borders* in this context.

- The *borders* of something are the edges of it.

READ FOR UNDERSTANDING

Summarize

ASK: What do you learn on pages 86–87? Use your own words to summarize. *(A spider builds a web by spinning threads. First it makes a "Y" shape, and then it spins threads to make the border, or frame, for the web.)*

DOK 2

READ FOR UNDERSTANDING

Summarize

MODEL SUMMARIZING

THINK ALOUD *I can pause here to summarize what I am reading. What are the most important ideas? I will tell them in my own words. A spider spins threads to make a web. First it uses non-sticky threads to make a framework and then a spiral.*

DOK 2

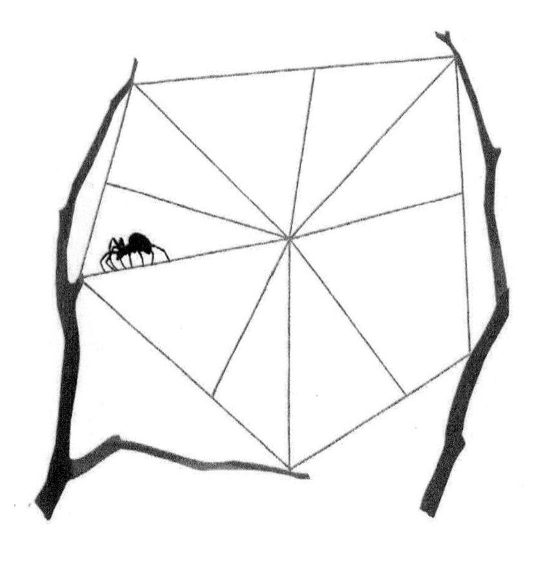

5 Spin threads from the center to the edges.

These lines form the framework for your web. They give you unsticky threads to walk on.

6 Make a spiral.

Make a spiral of silk.
So far, none of the threads you've spun are sticky.

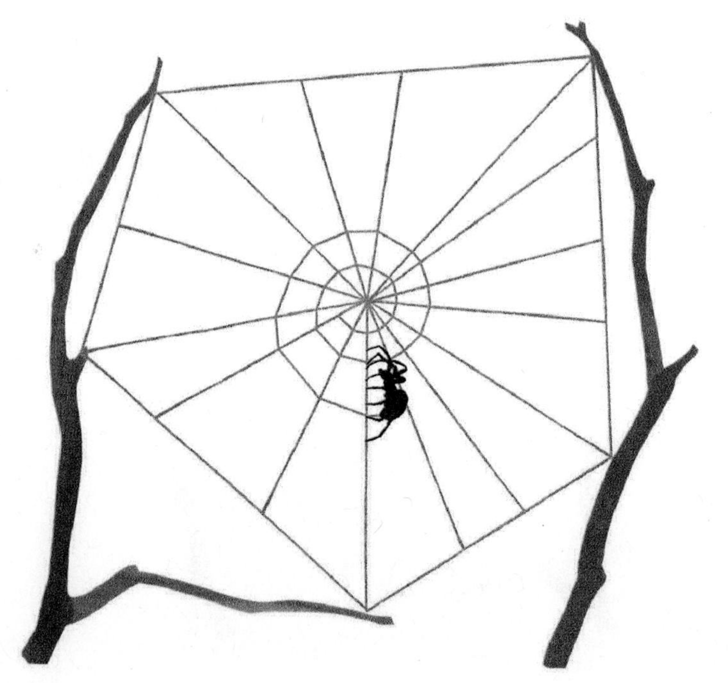

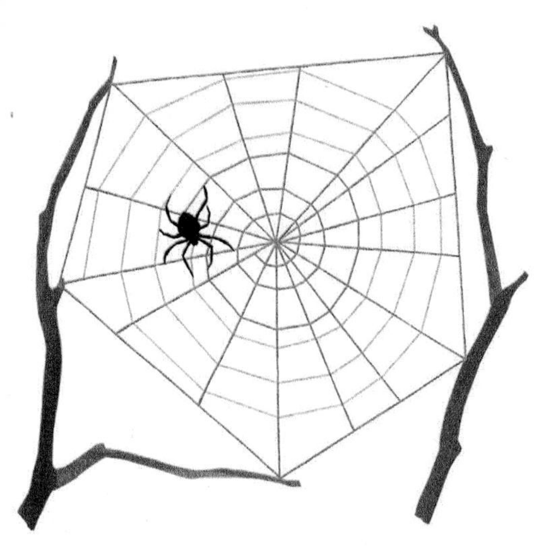

7 Get sticky.

Now work your way back to the center. Lay down sticky threads. The original spiral will be your path. You'll recycle it by eating it as you go.

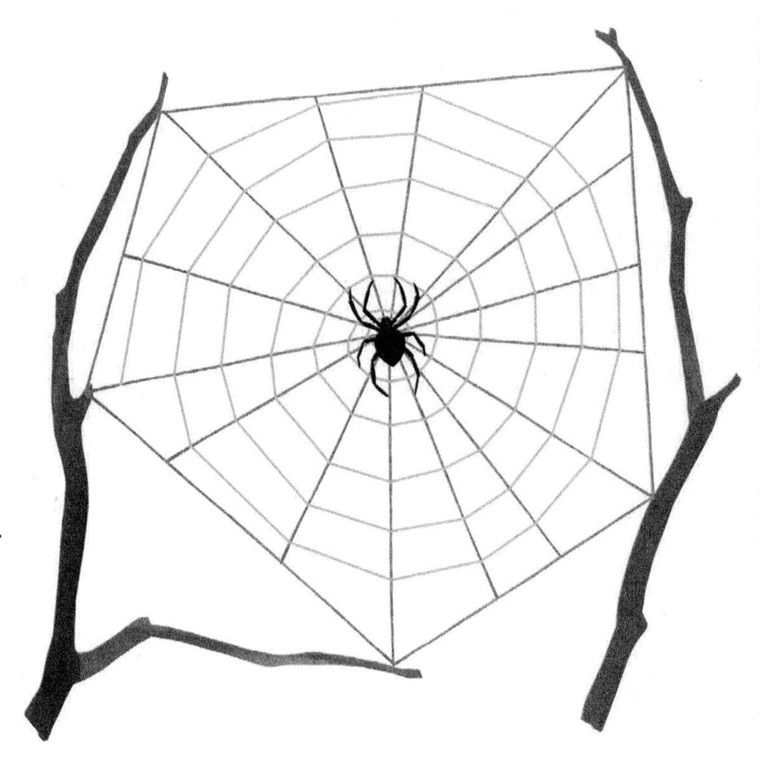

8 Wait for dinner.

Now you can rest. Sit in the center of your new web. Wait for an insect to blunder into your trap.

Notice & Note

Contrasts and Contradictions

- **Remind children that** when the author shows them something that contrasts or contradicts what they already know or have read, they should stop to notice and note. Tell them they should include the contrasts and contradictions when they summarize the text.
- **Have children explain** why they might use this strategy on pages 88–89. *(The spider first makes a web with threads that are not sticky. Then it spins it all over again using sticky threads and eats the non-sticky ones.)*
- **Remind them** of the Anchor Question: **What does this make me wonder about?** *(I wonder why the spider doesn't spin the web using sticky threads the first time. Why does it eat the first web?)*

DOK 2

 **READ FOR UNDERSTANDING**

Quick Teach Words

As needed to support comprehension, briefly explain the meaning of *blunder* in this context.

- If you *blunder* into something, you move into it by mistake or in a confused way.

READ FOR UNDERSTANDING

Phonics/Decoding in Context

Help children point to the word *fish*. Review that the letters *sh* stand for the sound /sh/. **Model blending** the sounds in the word: /f/ /ĭ/ /sh/, *fish*. Have children repeat.

ANNOTATION TIP: Have children circle *sh* in *fish* on pages 90–92.

TARGETED CLOSE READ

Text Organization

Have children reread pages 90–92 to analyze how the author organizes the text.

ASK: What does the author want you to understand from reading this text? *(the steps animals follow to survive in the wild)*

FOLLOW-UP: How does the author organize the information to help you understand this? *(The author organizes the information in steps that help you understand what happens first, next, and last, and that help you understand how one thing is connected to another.)*

DOK 3

How to Trap Fish Like a Humpback Whale

1 Find some fish.

The first step is locating a school of fish. Some of these schools include millions of fish.

2 Tell your friends.

Call any humpbacks in the area. Let them know you've located dinner.

90

3 Slap the surface.

Whacking the water with your tail frightens the fish. It makes them swim closer together. If you don't have a tail, ask one of the whales for help.

4 Swim in circles.

Join the whales in circling beneath the fish. Blow bubbles. Herd the fish together by swimming in smaller and smaller circles.

91

READ FOR UNDERSTANDING

Summarize

ASK: What do you learn about how humpback whales trap fish? Use your own words to summarize. *(Possible response: The whales find fish and call other whales. They slap their tails to scare the fish and make them swim near each other. Then the whales blow bubbles and circle the fish to bring the fish together.)*

DOK 2

 **READ FOR UNDERSTANDING**

Wrap Up

Revisit the predictions children made before reading. Have them confirm or correct their predictions using evidence from the text and pictures.

DOK 2

5 Gulp!

Take turns swimming up. Open your mouth wide. Swallow as many fish as you can in one gulp.

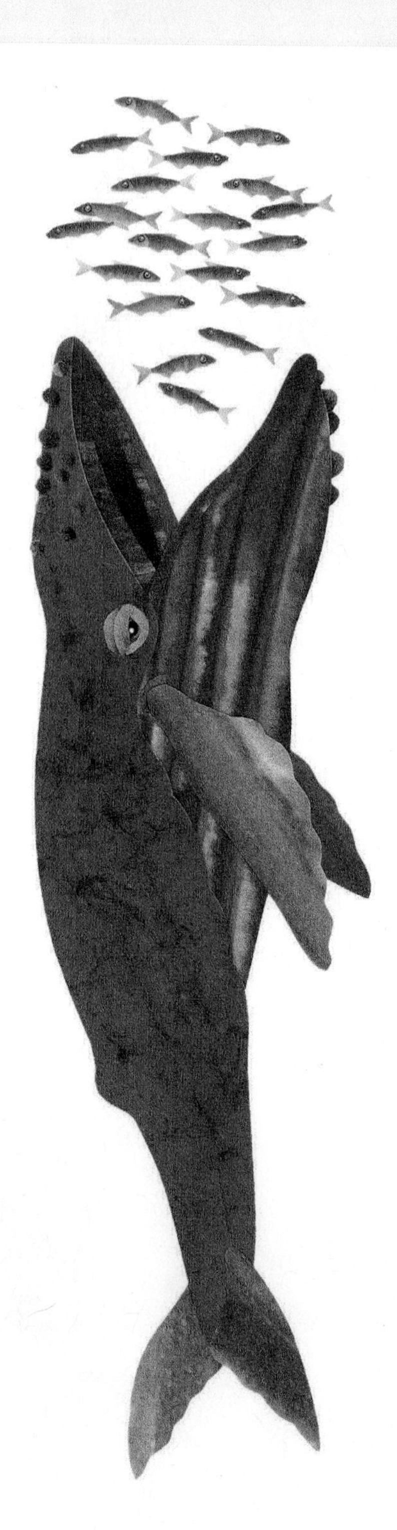

92

Respond to Reading

READ Together

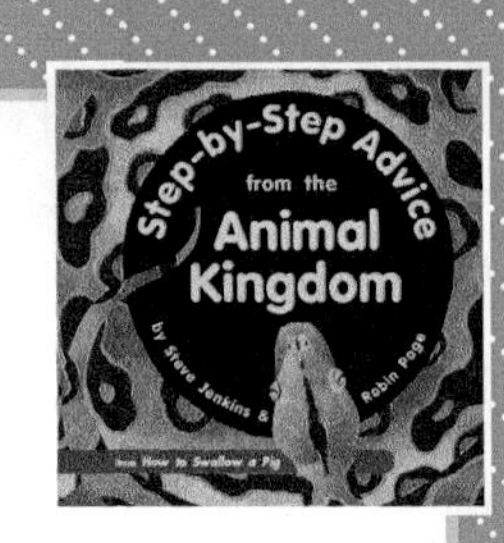

Use details from **Step-by-Step Advice from the Animal Kingdom** to answer these questions with a partner.

1. **Summarize** What are the most important ideas this text is about?

2. Which animal's body helps it the best? Use ideas from the text to tell why.

Talking Tip

Wait for your turn to talk. Explain your ideas and feelings clearly.

I feel that ______________.

93

Academic Discussion

Use the TURN AND TALK routine. Remind children to follow agreed-upon rules for discussion, such as listening carefully, waiting for their turn to talk, and explaining their ideas and feelings clearly.

Possible responses:

1. *Animals use their bodies in different ways to get food or to protect themselves. Armadillos run, dig, swim, and hide to stay safe. Spiders make sticky webs to catch food. Whales work together to find fish, herd them together, and eat them.* DOK 2
2. *The spider; it works alone to use its body to make a sticky web to catch food.* DOK 2

Cite Text Evidence

READ Together

Write a Fact

PROMPT You learned a lot about animals in **Step-by-Step Advice from the Animal Kingdom**. What was the most interesting fact?

PLAN First, draw a picture of the animal and write words to tell about the most interesting fact.

94

Write About Reading

- **Read aloud** the prompt.
- **Lead a discussion** in which children summarize the facts they learned and share their ideas about which animal fact they think is the most interesting. Tell children to use text evidence to support their ideas.
- Then read aloud the Plan section. Have children use ideas from the discussion in their drawings and writings.

DOK 3

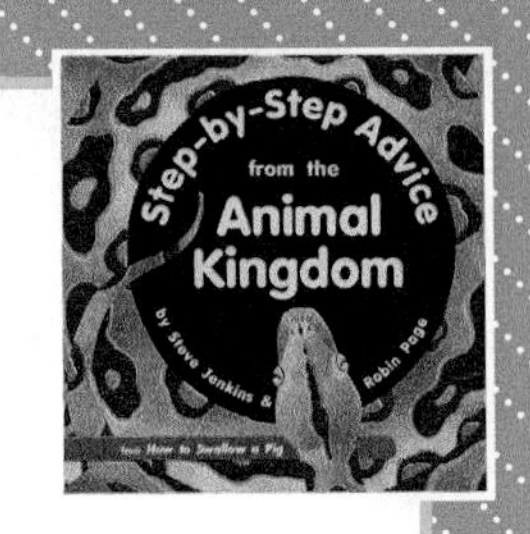

WRITE Now write your fact. Use your picture and notes for ideas. Remember to:

- Tell true information.
- Be sure your sentence tells a complete idea.

Responses may vary.

Write About Reading

- **Read aloud** the Write section.
- **Encourage children** to reread the text to check that their facts are correct. Remind them that sentences begin with a capital letter, end with a period, and tell a complete idea.

DOK 3

Independent Close Reading

Have children close read and annotate "Pop-Up Armadillo" on their own during small-group or independent work time. As needed, **use the Scaffolded Support notes** that follow to guide children who need additional help.

Scaffolded Support

As needed, remind children that:

- they can use their own words to summarize the most important ideas in the text.
- authors sometimes help them understand a topic by explaining the steps they need to follow in order.

DOK 3

Prepare to Read

GENRE STUDY **Procedural texts** tell how to do or make something.

MAKE A PREDICTION Preview **Pop-Up Armadillo**. Look at the features, like the numbers and pictures. What do you think you will learn?

I will learn the steps for making a pop-up armadillo.

SET A PURPOSE Read to find out how to make a pop-up armadillo. Find clues that the text is organized to explain the steps in order.

Pop-Up Armadillo

READ Circle words and other things that show the order of the steps.

You can make a pop-up armadillo!

1 First, get what you see in **1** at the top.

2 Then color an armadillo.
Do not make it too big.
Do not make it too little.
Make it fit. ▶

Close Reading Tip

Mark important ideas with *.

CHECK MY UNDERSTANDING

What is the most important idea in this part?

Make an armadillo picture the right size.

97

Scaffolded Support

As needed, guide children to:

- look for clue words such as *first*, *next*, and *last* and numbered items that show the order of the steps.
- use their own words to tell the steps in order.
- ask themselves, *Is this detail important for making the pop-up armadillo?* as they mark ideas in the text and pictures.

DOK 3

READ What are the most important ideas in this part? Tell why you think the author wrote **Pop-Up Armadillo**.

3 Cut out the armadillo.
Do not cut the border!
Look at **3** on page 97 to see how.

4 Then bend back the top border.
Color all of it to make it look great!

5 Last, cut up paper to make grass.
Add it to the pop-up.

Now tell your classmates about your armadillo!

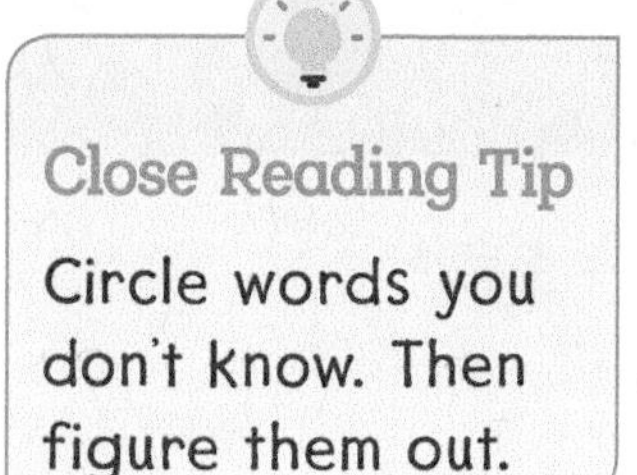

Close Reading Tip

Circle words you don't know. Then figure them out.

Scaffolded Support

As needed, guide children to:

- think about the information they would really need to keep in mind if they were making the pop-up armadillo.
- wonder what would happen if the person making the pop-up armadillo did not know the order of the steps.
- ask themselves questions about the words they do not know and use clues from the words and pictures to figure out their meaning.

DOK 2

CHECK MY UNDERSTANDING

Why did the author write the steps in order?

so you would not get mixed up and to help you make it correctly

Cite Text Evidence

WRITE ABOUT IT In your own words, write the most important ideas you learned about making a pop-up animal. Use words like **first, next, then,** and **last** to help you tell things in order.

First, make a picture of an animal on a paper plate. Next, cut out most of it. Then bend it back. Last, decorate it.

Scaffolded Support

As needed, guide children to begin by summarizing the directions in their own words. Then help them use sequence words to write each step.

DOK 3

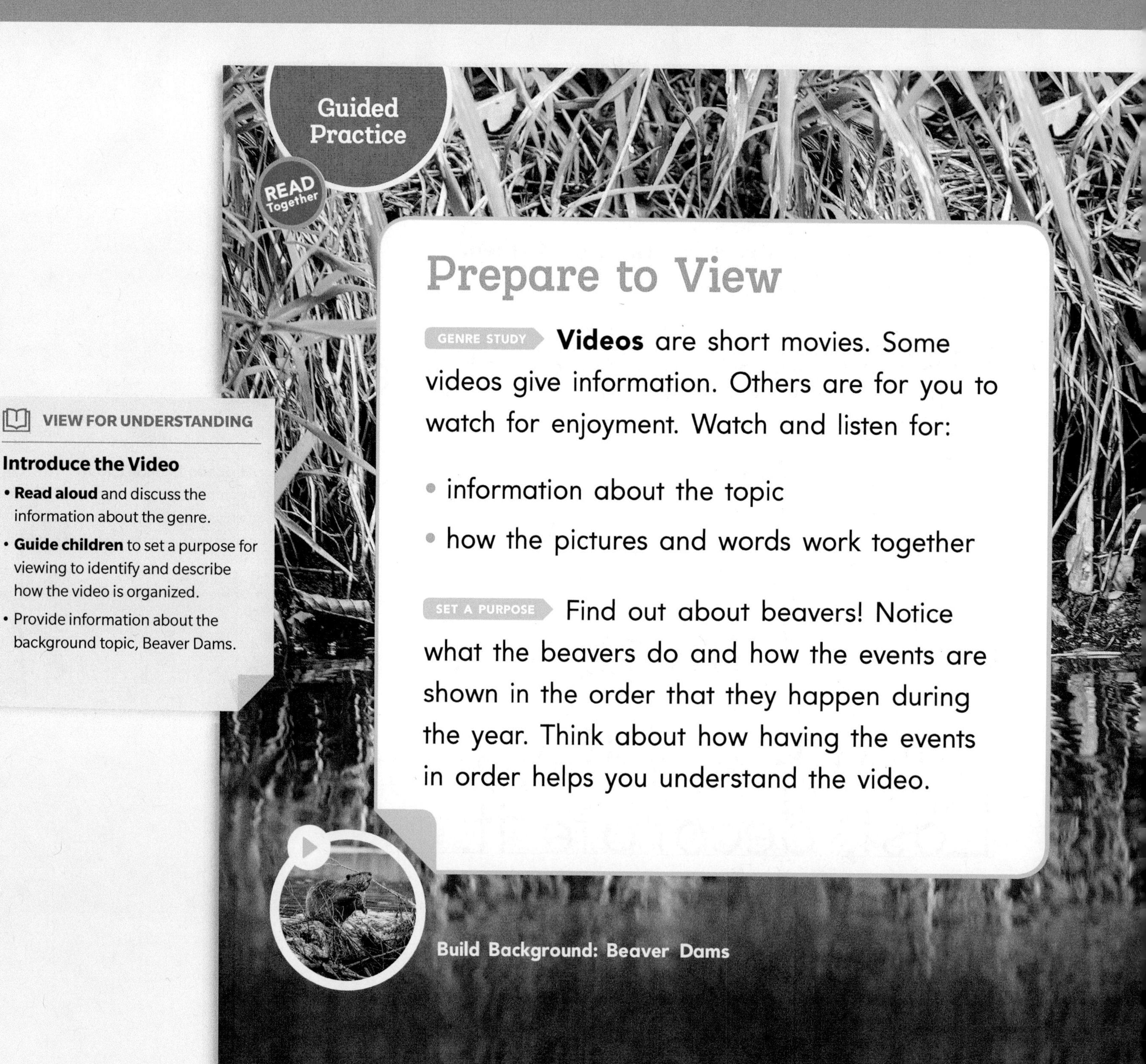

Prepare to View

GENRE STUDY **Videos** are short movies. Some videos give information. Others are for you to watch for enjoyment. Watch and listen for:

- information about the topic
- how the pictures and words work together

SET A PURPOSE Find out about beavers! Notice what the beavers do and how the events are shown in the order that they happen during the year. Think about how having the events in order helps you understand the video.

Build Background: Beaver Dams

VIEW FOR UNDERSTANDING

Introduce the Video

- **Read aloud** and discuss the information about the genre.
- **Guide children** to set a purpose for viewing to identify and describe how the video is organized.
- Provide information about the background topic, Beaver Dams.

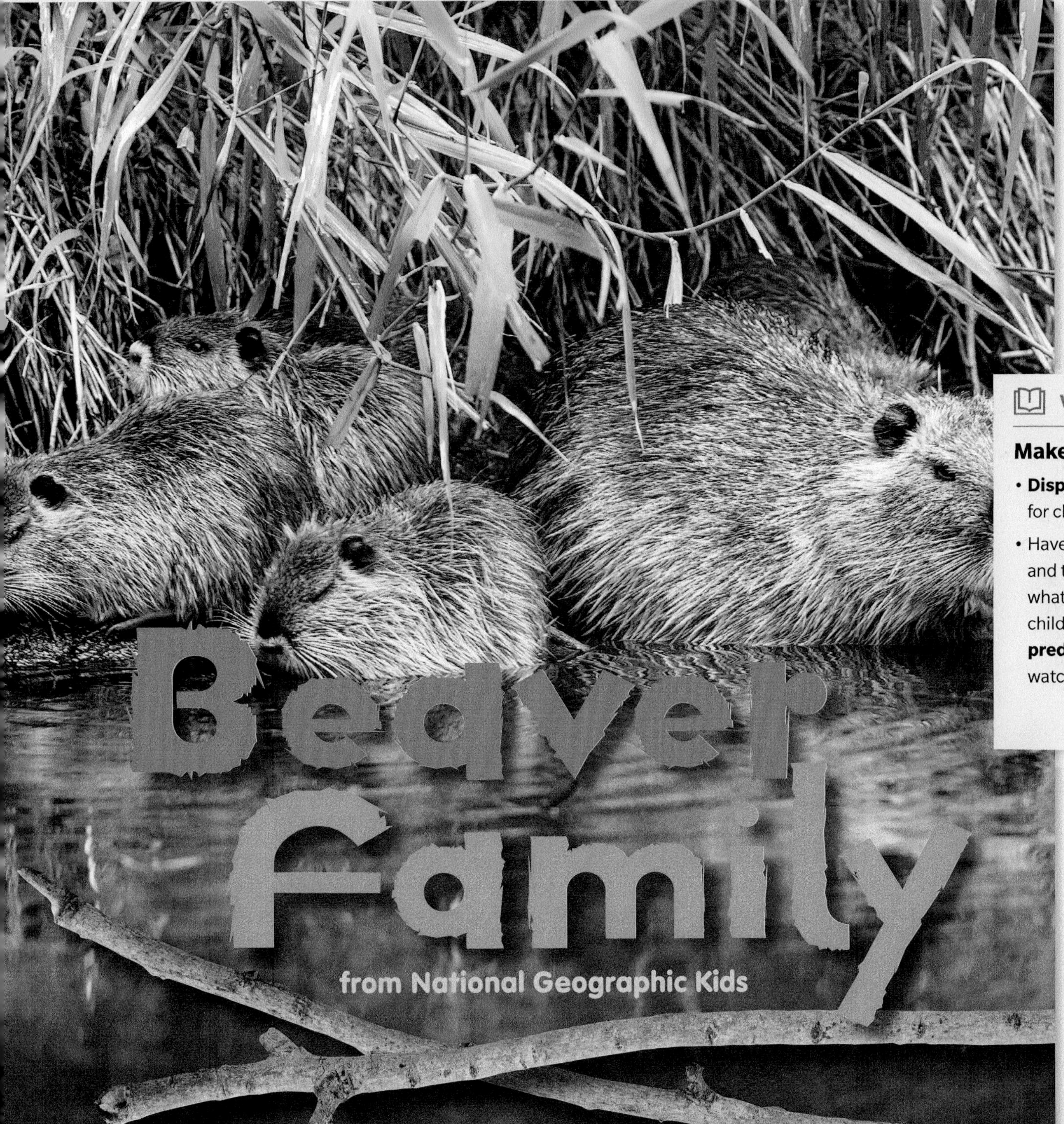

VIEW FOR UNDERSTANDING

Make Predictions

- **Display** the cover of *Beaver Family* for children.
- Have them **use prior knowledge** and the opening picture to predict what the video will be about. Tell children they will **return to their predictions** after they finish watching the video.

DOK 2

VIEW FOR UNDERSTANDING

Chronological Order

ASK: How is the information about the beavers organized? *(The things beavers do throughout the year are shown in the order in which they happen.)*

FOLLOW-UP: Why do you think the video is organized this way? *(Possible response: So the viewer can understand what the beavers do during each season.)*

DOK 3

As You View Notice how the video has a beginning, middle, and end. The events happen in order. How does this help you understand the video? Use the words and pictures to find out what the beavers do before, during, and after winter.

Respond to Media

Use details from **Beaver Family** to answer these questions with a partner.

1. **Chronological Order** What important things do beavers do before winter? What do they do during winter? Then what do they do in the spring?

2. How does a beaver use its body to build a dam?

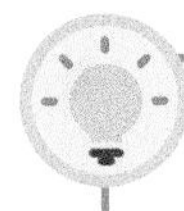

Listening Tip

Listen carefully. Make connections. How is what your partner says like other things you know?

Academic Discussion

Use the TURN AND TALK routine. Remind children to follow agreed-upon rules for discussion, such as listening carefully and making connections between your and your partner's ideas.

Possible responses:

1. *Before winter, beavers build a home and collect branches to eat during the winter. In spring, beavers work to keep the dam in place.* DOK 2
2. *It swims and carries branches into the water. Its skin flaps help it carry branches without swallowing water.* DOK 2

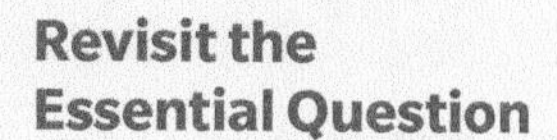

Revisit the Essential Question

- **Read aloud** the Essential Question.
- **Remind children** that in this module, they read different texts about how animals live.
- **Have children** choose one of the activities to show what they learned in this module.

Animal Dos and Don'ts

- **Help children** revisit the texts and review the different animals they read about. Have them choose the animal they think is most interesting to write about.
- **Tell children** to emphasize the words *Do* and *Don't* as they share their ideas with their partners.

DOK 2

READ Together

Let's Wrap Up!

Essential Question

How do animals' bodies help them?

Pick one of these activities to show what you have learned about the topic.

1. Animal Dos and Don'ts

Pick an animal you have read about. Talk to a partner. Describe what the animal should do and should not do to survive. Complete these sentences:

Do ________.

Don't ________.

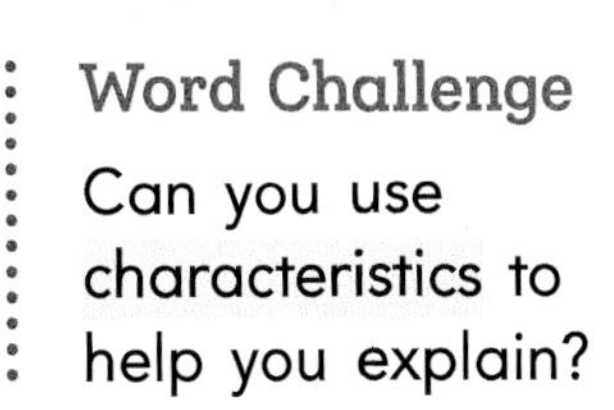

2. Animal Babies

Draw a picture of one of the animals you read about. Write to explain how the mom or dad animal would take care of the babies. Share your writing with classmates.

Word Challenge

Can you use characteristics to help you explain?

My Notes

105

Animal Babies

- **Guide children** to think about what baby animals need to grow and stay safe.
- **Help them** to explain the meaning of the word *characteristics* in their own words before they begin to write.

DOK 2

Brainstorm and Plan

Have children use the My Notes space to jot down ideas for their chosen activity. Remind them to refer back to their notes as they complete the activity.

Introduce the Topic

- **Read aloud** the module title, *Better Together.*
- **Tell children** that in this module they will be reading texts about being good citizens.
- **Have children** share prior knowledge about the topic or word associations for being good citizens. Record their ideas in a web.

Discuss the Quotation

- **Read aloud** the quotation by Confucius.
- **Lead a discussion** in which children try to explain the quote in their own words. Explain the meaning as needed: *Treat others the way you would like to be treated.*

ASK: How have you treated someone the way you would like to be treated? *(Accept reasonable responses.)*

MODULE 4

Better Together

"What you do not want done to yourself, do not do to others."

—Confucius

106

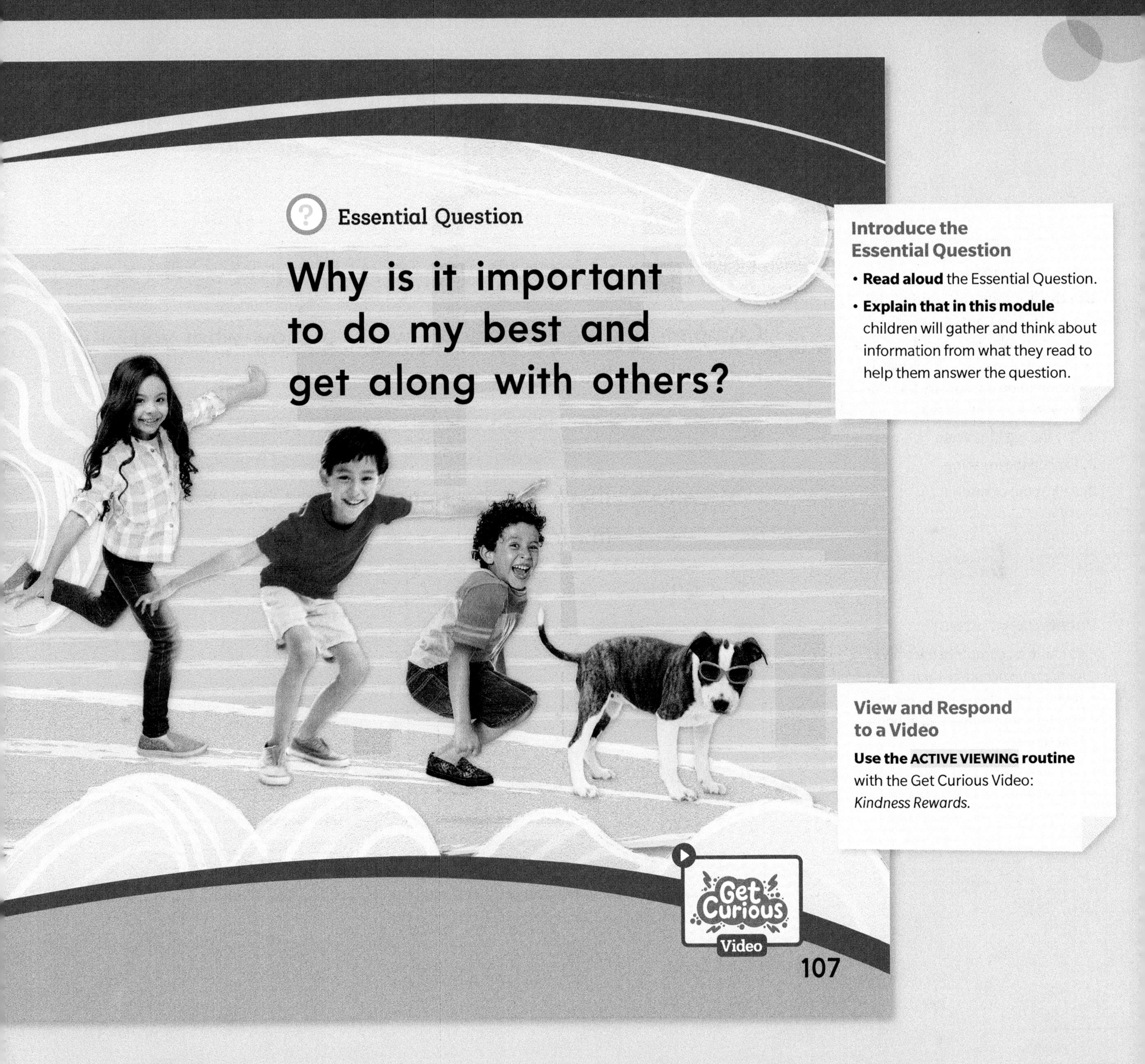

Introduce the Essential Question

- **Read aloud** the Essential Question.
- **Explain that in this module** children will gather and think about information from what they read to help them answer the question.

View and Respond to a Video

Use the ACTIVE VIEWING routine with the Get Curious Video: *Kindness Rewards.*

Big Idea Words

Use the VOCABULARY routine and the Vocabulary Cards to introduce the Big Idea Words *honest, sport,* and *courtesy*. You may wish to display the corresponding Vocabulary Card for each word as you discuss it.

1. Say the Big Idea Word.
2. Explain the meaning.
3. Talk about examples.

Vocabulary Network

- **As children complete** the activity for *honest,* encourage them to think about times when they have been truthful about something at home or at school.

Words About Being Good Citizens

Complete the Vocabulary Network to show what you know about the words.

honest	
Meaning: If you are an **honest** person, you tell the truth.	
Synonyms and Antonyms	Drawing

108

sport

Meaning: A good **sport** plays fair and gets along with others.

Synonyms and Antonyms	Drawing

courtesy

Meaning: If you do something as a **courtesy**, you do it to be kind or polite.

Synonyms and Antonyms	Drawing

Vocabulary Network

- **Prompt children** to think about what they do to be a good *sport* when they win or lose a game.
- **As children complete** the activity for *courtesy*, prompt them to think of things they do and say in order to be polite.

READ FOR UNDERSTANDING

Introduce the Text

- **Read aloud** the title, *Good Sports.* Tell children that it is opinion writing. Ask them to recall what they know about opinion writing. *(It tells what an author thinks about a topic, and gives reasons for the author's ideas.)*
- Guide children to **set a purpose.**
- **Read the text** with children.

DOK 3

READ FOR UNDERSTANDING

Ideas and Support

ASK: What does the girl want you to think about being a good sport? *(She wants you to think it's important to be a good sport.)*

ANNOTATION TIP: Have children underline the sentence that tells the girl's opinion.

FOLLOW-UP: What reasons does the girl give to support her opinion? *(Everyone has fun when good sports play fair. Good sports make good teammates.)*

DOK 2

Short Read

READ Together

Is it good to be a good sport? Find out one person's opinion.

I think it's important to be a good sport. Here's why! Good sports play fair. They follow the rules. Everyone has more fun when a game is fair. Also, good sports are good teammates. They take turns. They try hard and work together to score points. They cheer for others.

Finally, good sports are nice to be with. They don't get grouchy about who wins or loses. They think it's fun just to play! So, be a good sport. You will have fun, and others will, too!

111

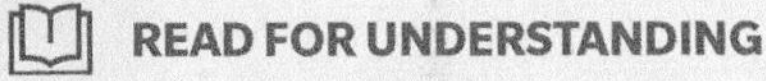

READ FOR UNDERSTANDING

Ideas and Support

ASK: Do you agree or disagree with the girl's opinion? Why? *(Accept reasonable responses.)*

DOK 2

READ FOR UNDERSTANDING

ANNOTATION TIP: Ask children to circle each reason the girl gives for why it is important to be a good sport.

Introduce the Text

- **Read aloud** and discuss the information about the genre.
- **Guide children** to set a purpose for reading to practice evaluating important ideas.
- **Provide information** about the author, Jane Medina.
- **Tell children** to look for and think about the Power Words as they read.

Guided Practice

Prepare to Read

GENRE STUDY **Informational text** is nonfiction. It gives facts about a topic or real people. Look for:

- photographs of a real person
- facts about real events
- pictures with labels

POWER WORDS

- team
- equipment
- coach
- rules
- goal
- fan

SET A PURPOSE Think about the author's words as you read. Then decide, or **evaluate**, which details are the most important to help you understand the text.

Meet Jane Medina.

112

Make Predictions

- **Page through** the beginning of *Goal!* with children.
- Have them **use prior knowledge** and the photos and illustrations to predict what the text will be about. Tell children they will **return to their predictions** after they finish reading the text.

DOK 2

Concept Words

As children read *Goal!*, they may see familiar words from their speaking and listening vocabularies that they may not know how to read yet. Write these words on the board, read them aloud, and discuss their meanings as needed.

- ball
- dribble
- game
- goalie
- hands
- number
- practice
- referee
- soccer
- uniform
- Collette Mora
- Brittney
- Yvonne

READ FOR UNDERSTANDING

ASK: Who is the girl in the photo and the illustration? *(Colette Mora as an adult and as a young girl)*

FOLLOW-UP: Why do you think the author shows Colette Mora in these two ways? *(The author wants to let the reader know that Colette Mora is a real person and show what she might have looked like when she started playing soccer.)*

ANNOTATION TIP: Have children label the pictures of Colette on pages 114 and 115.

DOK 2

TARGETED CLOSE READ

Point of View

Have children reread pages 114–115 to analyze point of view.

ASK: Who is the narrator? *(Colette, the person the text is about.)*

FOLLOW-UP: How do you know? *(She introduces herself and uses the words I and my.)*

ANNOTATION TIP: Have children circle the words that help them understand who the narrator is.

DOK 3

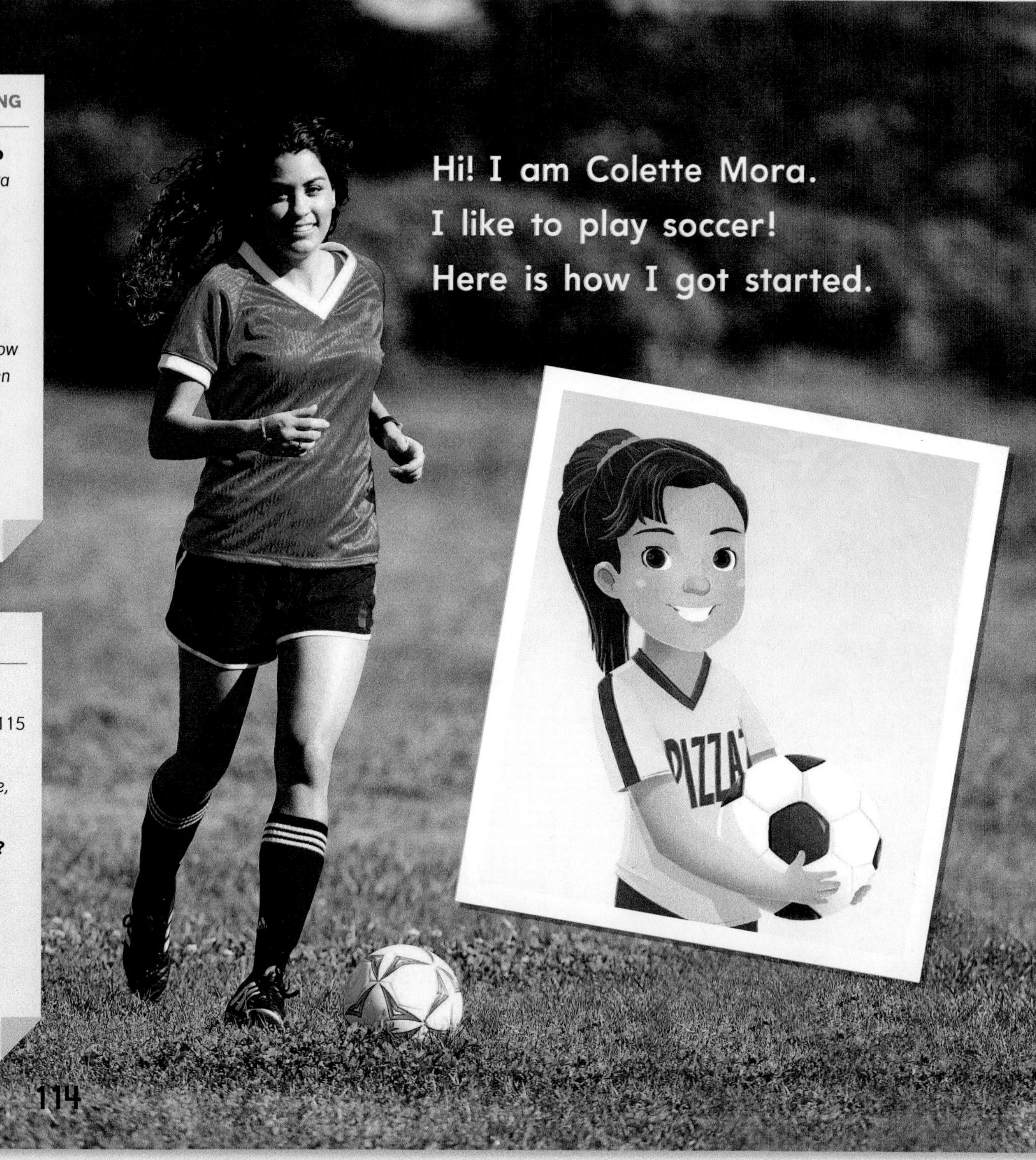

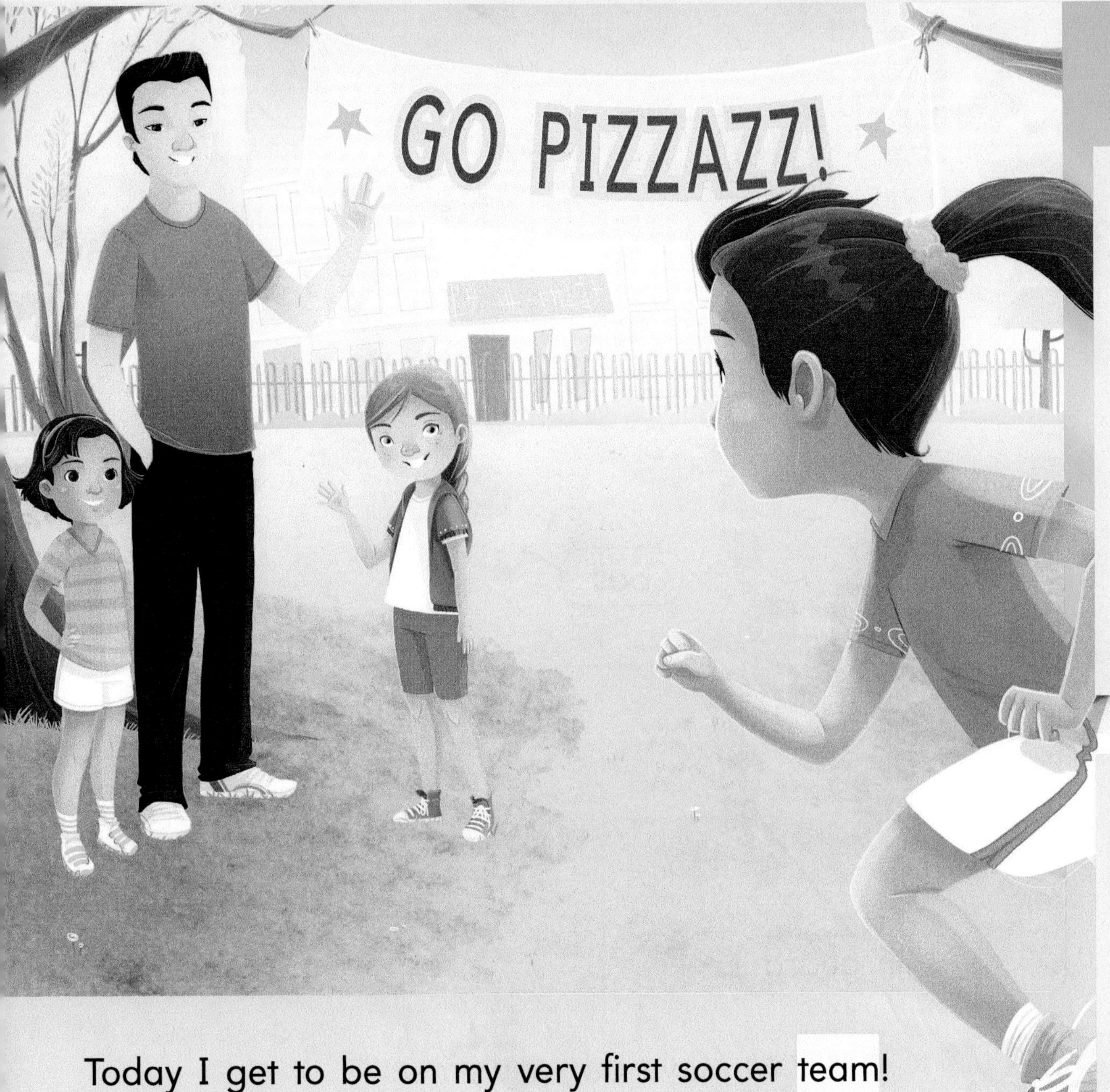

Today I get to be on my very first soccer team!
I see my twin Yvonne and my friend Brittney.

115

READ FOR UNDERSTANDING

Evaluate

MODEL EVALUATING

THINK ALOUD *When I read, I think about the author's words. Then I evaluate, or decide, which ideas are important to know and which are just interesting. I know that this text is about how Colette Mora started playing soccer. The idea that Colette gets on her first soccer team is an important detail. The details about her twin and her friend are interesting, but they don't help tell how Colette got started in soccer.*

DOK 3

READ FOR UNDERSTANDING

Quick Teach Words

As needed to support comprehension, briefly explain the meaning of the word *twin* in this context.

- A *twin* is one of two children who were born at the same time to the same mother.

READ FOR UNDERSTANDING

Phonics/Decoding in Context

Have children point to the word *such* on page 116. Remind them that the consonants *ch* together stand for one sound, /ch/. **Model blending** the sounds in the word: /s/ /ŭ/ /ch/, *such*. Have children repeat.

ANNOTATION TIP: Have children circle *ch* in the word.

READ FOR UNDERSTANDING

ASK: What information do the labels give? *(the kinds of equipment needed to play soccer)*

ANNOTATION TIP: Have children circle the labels that name soccer equipment.

FOLLOW-UP: Why does the author include a label for the girl's smile? *(Possible responses: to show that Colette is happy to be learning about soccer; to show that having a positive attitude is importat when playing sports)*

DOK2

We have our equipment.
We will have such fun!

116

Mr. Chan will coach us.

"Pick a number for your uniform," he tells us.

Yvonne picks six.

Brittney picks ten.

I pick 12.

117

READ FOR UNDERSTANDING

Quick Teach Words

As needed to support comprehension, briefly explain the meaning of the abbreviation *Mr.*

- *Mr.* is used as a title before the name of a man, as in *Mr. Chan*.

READ FOR UNDERSTANDING

Phonics/Decoding in Context

Have children point to the word *coach*. Remind them that together, the consonants *ch* stand for one sound, /ch/. **Model blending** the sounds in the word: /k/ /ō/ /ch/, *coach*. Have children repeat.

ANNOTATION TIP: Have children circle *ch* in the word.

READ FOR UNDERSTANDING

ASK: What do you think the goalie's job is? *(to stop the ball from going into the net)*

FOLLOW-UP: What clues help you understand this? *(The text says that the goalie is the only one on the team that can use her hands; the picture shows a girl holding her hands up, ready to stop a ball.)*

ANNOTATION TIP: Have children circle the goalie in the picture.

DOK 2

I am at my first practice.
Coach tells us the rules.
"Kick the ball.
Do not use your hands.
But the goalie *can* use her
hands to get the ball."

118

"The rules help you play fair and be safe.
Then we can *all* have fun!"

119

READ FOR UNDERSTANDING

Evaluate

MODEL EVALUATING

THINK ALOUD *After I read these pages, I think about the author's words. I evaluate which details are important to remember about how Colette got started playing soccer. At her first practice, Colette learns the rules. Rules are important to know if you want to have fun. So learning the rules is an important detail to know about how to get started playing soccer.*

DOK 3

Notice & Note

Word Gaps

- **Remind children** that when an author uses a word or phrase they don't know, they can ask themselves questions to understand the meaning. Explain that understanding the meaning of words can help them evaluate important details.
- **Have children** explain why they might use this strategy if they didn't know the word *dribble* on page 120. *(I think about whether I know this word from someplace else. I think about how the word is related to soccer. I can look for clues about its meaning in the sentences.)*

ANNOTATION TIP: Have children underline the word *dribble*.

- **Remind them** of the Anchor Question: **Can I find clues in the sentences to help me understand the word?** *(The words "Kick it a little. Then run to it." are clues that* dribble *means "to move a ball by kicking it.")*

DOK 2

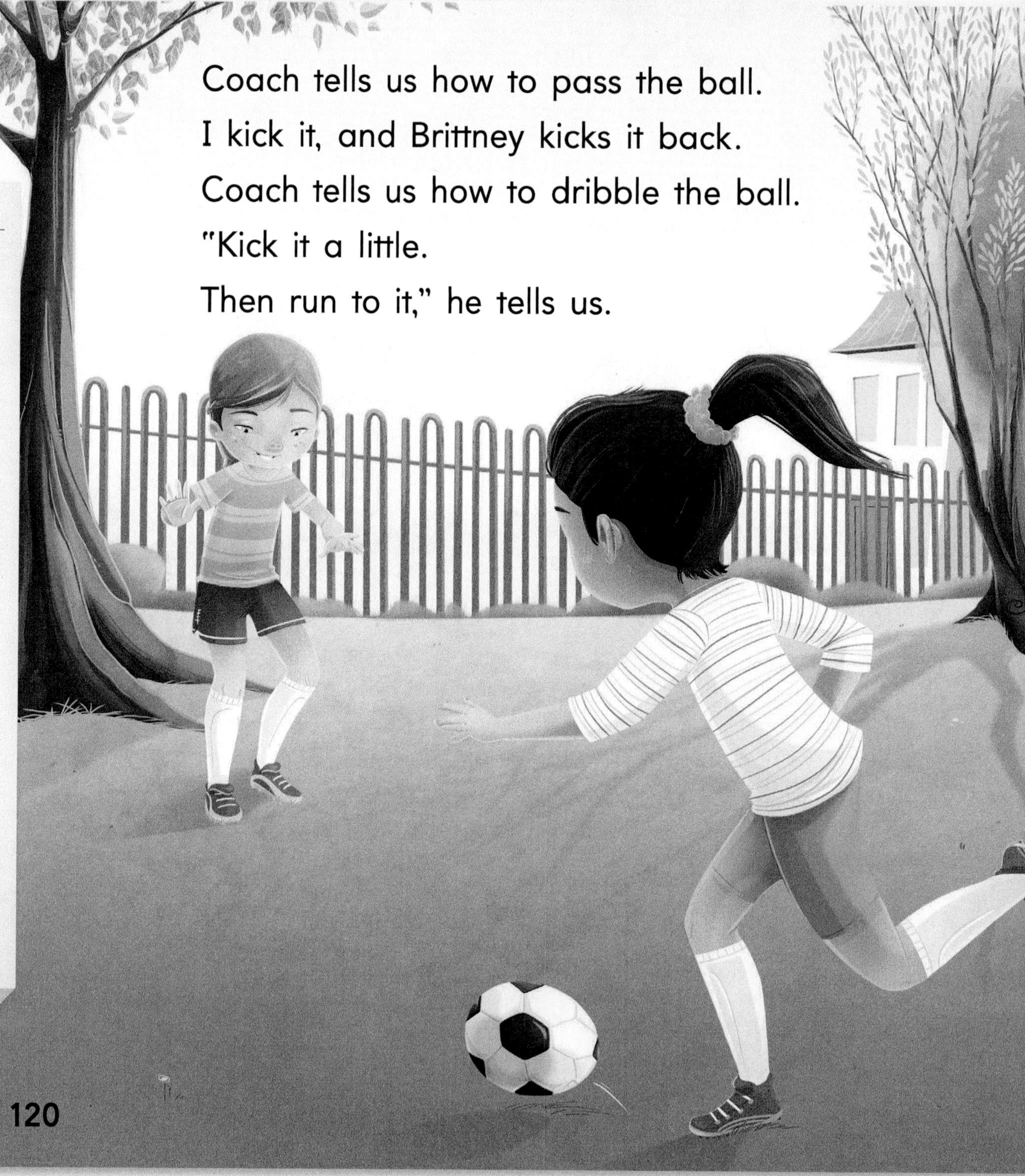

Coach tells us how to pass the ball.
I kick it, and Brittney kicks it back.
Coach tells us how to dribble the ball.
"Kick it a little.
Then run to it," he tells us.

120

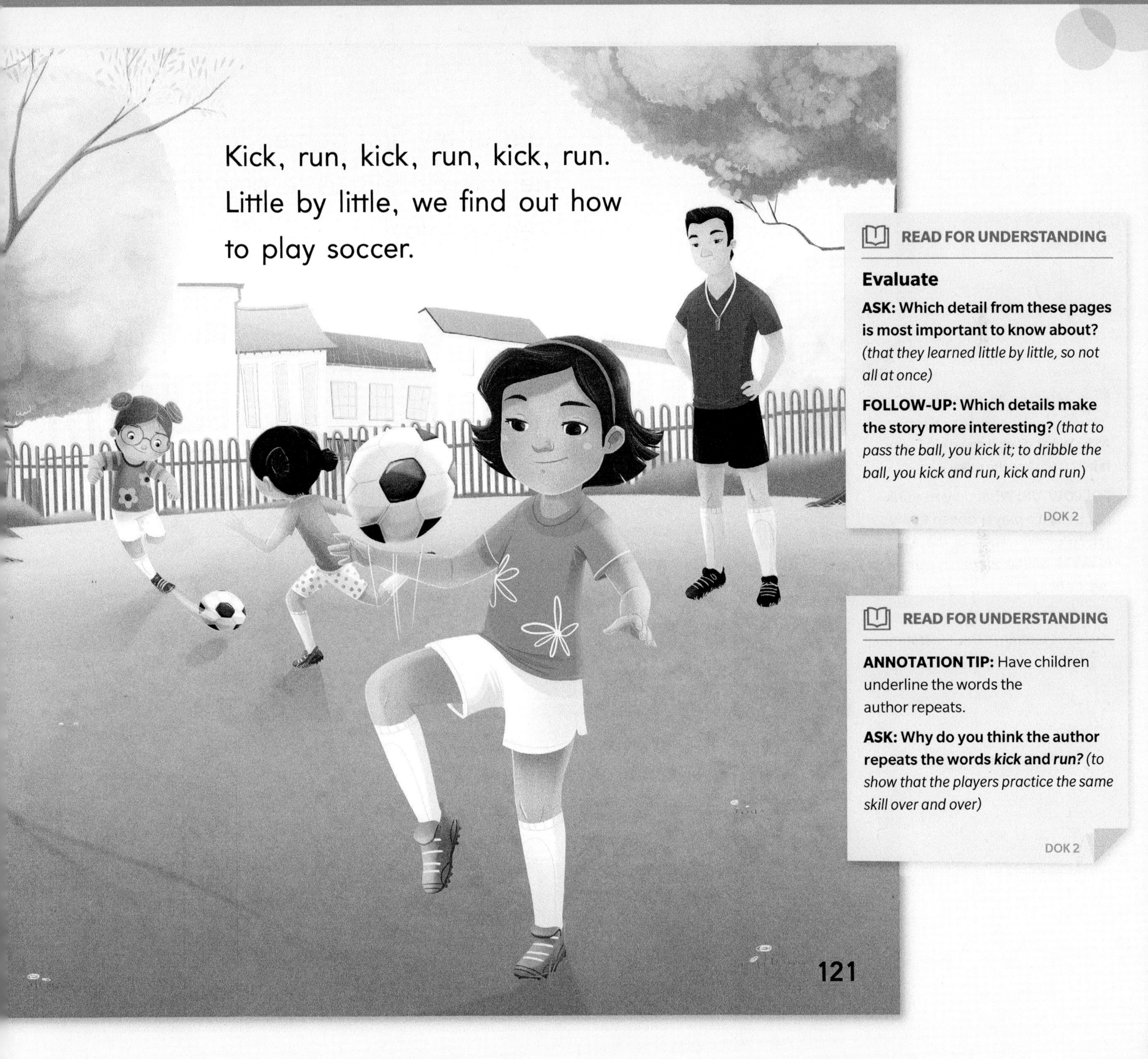

READ FOR UNDERSTANDING

Evaluate

ASK: Which detail from these pages is most important to know about? *(that they learned little by little, so not all at once)*

FOLLOW-UP: Which details make the story more interesting? *(that to pass the ball, you kick it; to dribble the ball, you kick and run, kick and run)*

DOK 2

READ FOR UNDERSTANDING

ANNOTATION TIP: Have children underline the words the author repeats.

ASK: Why do you think the author repeats the words *kick* and *run*? *(to show that the players practice the same skill over and over)*

DOK 2

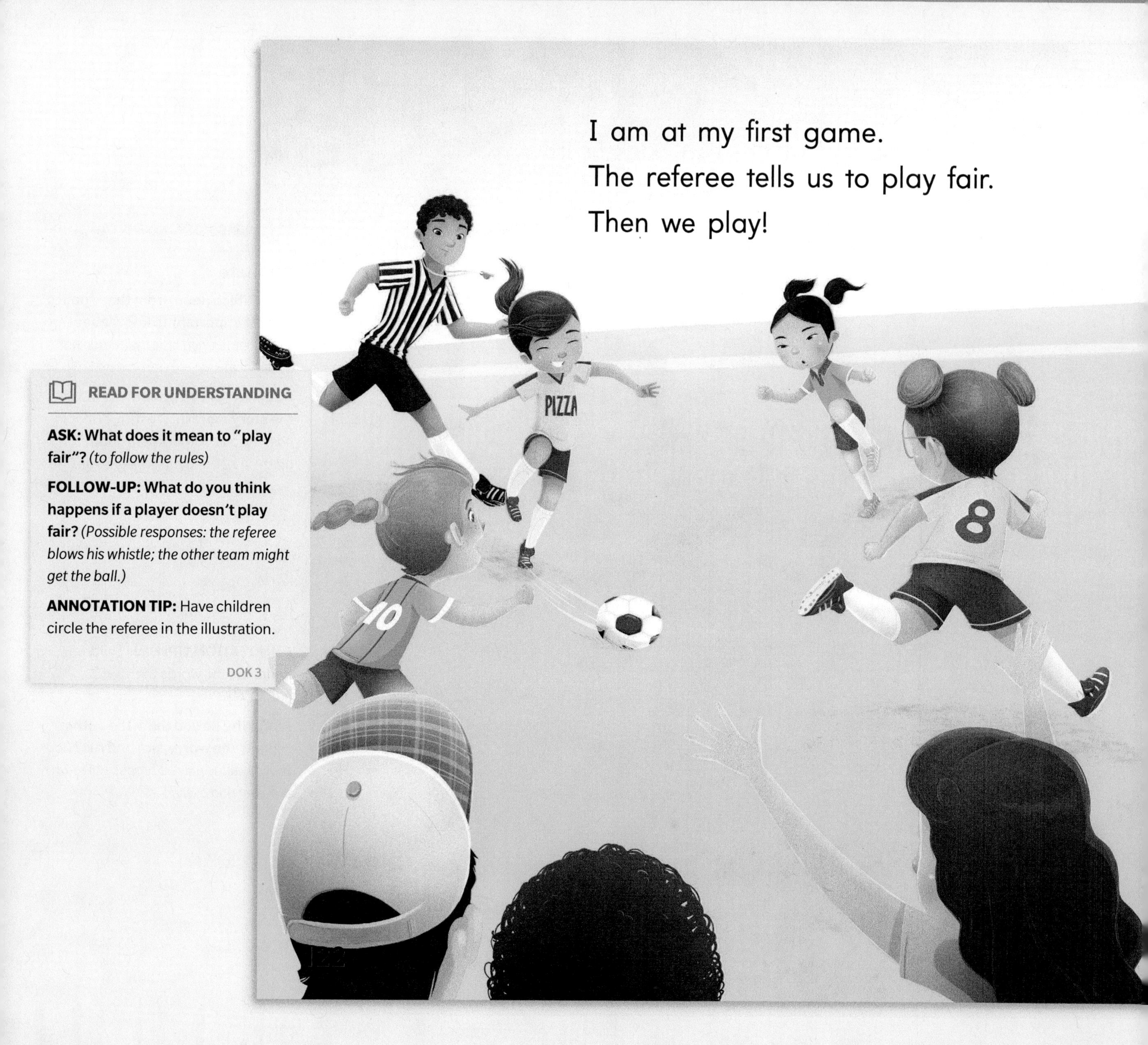

I am at my first game.
The referee tells us to play fair.
Then we play!

READ FOR UNDERSTANDING

ASK: What does it mean to "play fair"? *(to follow the rules)*

FOLLOW-UP: What do you think happens if a player doesn't play fair? *(Possible responses: the referee blows his whistle; the other team might get the ball.)*

ANNOTATION TIP: Have children circle the referee in the illustration.

DOK 3

I pass the ball to Brittney.
She kicks it to Yvonne.
Kick, pass, kick, pass.

123

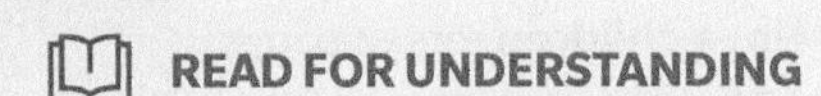

READ FOR UNDERSTANDING

ASK: How do the players show teamwork? *(They pass and kick the ball to each other.)*

ANNOTATION TIP: Have children draw a line from player to player to show the path the ball took.

DOK 2

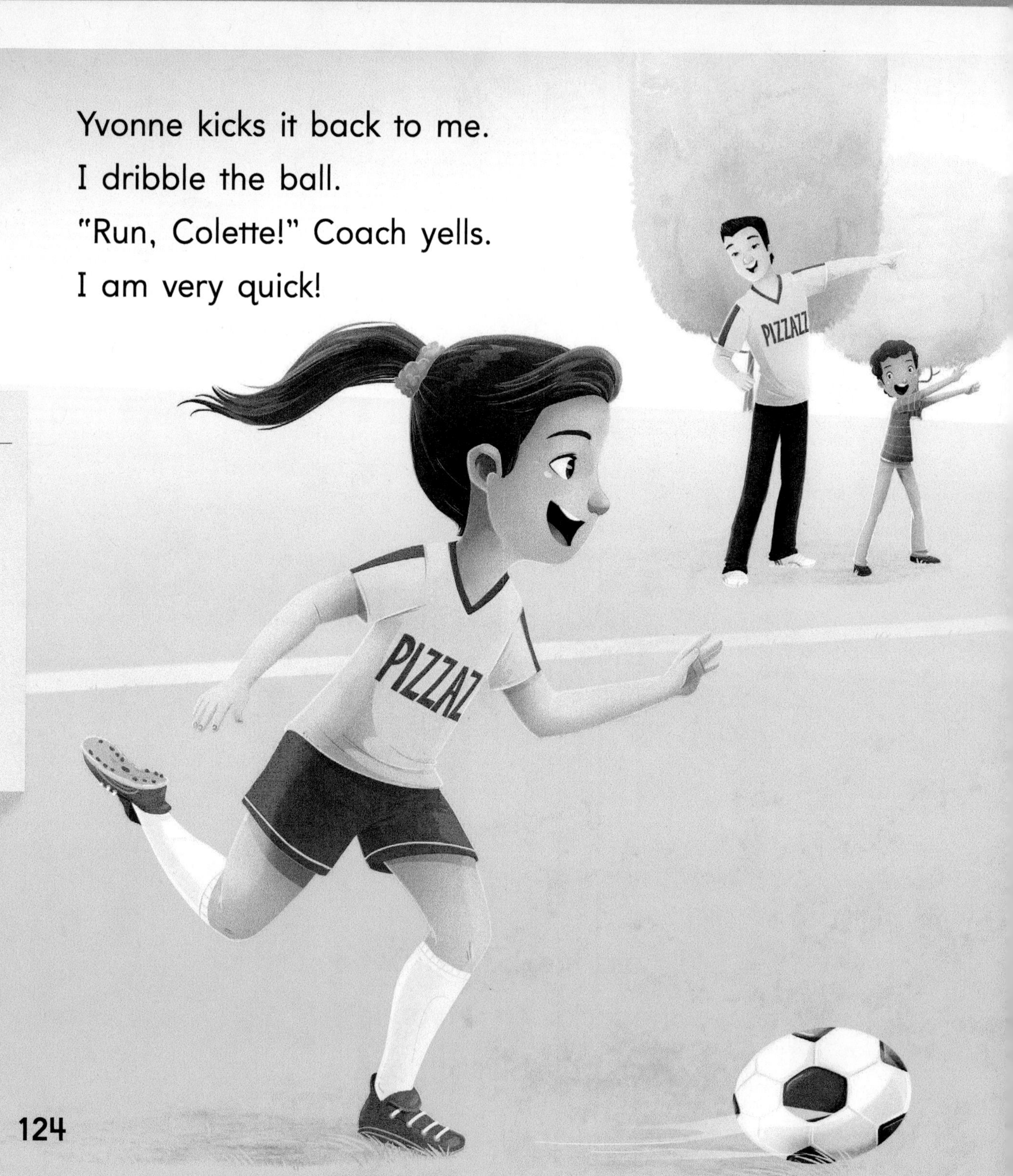

Yvonne kicks it back to me.
I dribble the ball.
"Run, Colette!" Coach yells.
I am very quick!

124

TARGETED CLOSE READ

Point of View

Have children reread pages 124–125 to analyze point of view.

ASK: From which point of view is this story told? *(first person)*

FOLLOW-UP: Which words help you understand this? *(me, I, my)*

ANNOTATION TIP: Have children circle the words that help them understand that the text is told from the first-person point of view.

DOK 3

The goalie runs to get the ball.
I kick it at the net. Then . . .
GOAL!
I got my very first goal!

125

READ FOR UNDERSTANDING

ASK: Why does the author label the net and goalie? *(to help the reader understand that a player scores a goal by kicking the ball past the goalie into the net)*

FOLLOW-UP: Why does the author show the word *GOAL* in bold and capital letters? *(to let the reader know how excited the girls were that Colette got a goal)*

ANNOTATION TIP: Have children draw a line to show the path the ball took from Colette to the net.

DOK 2

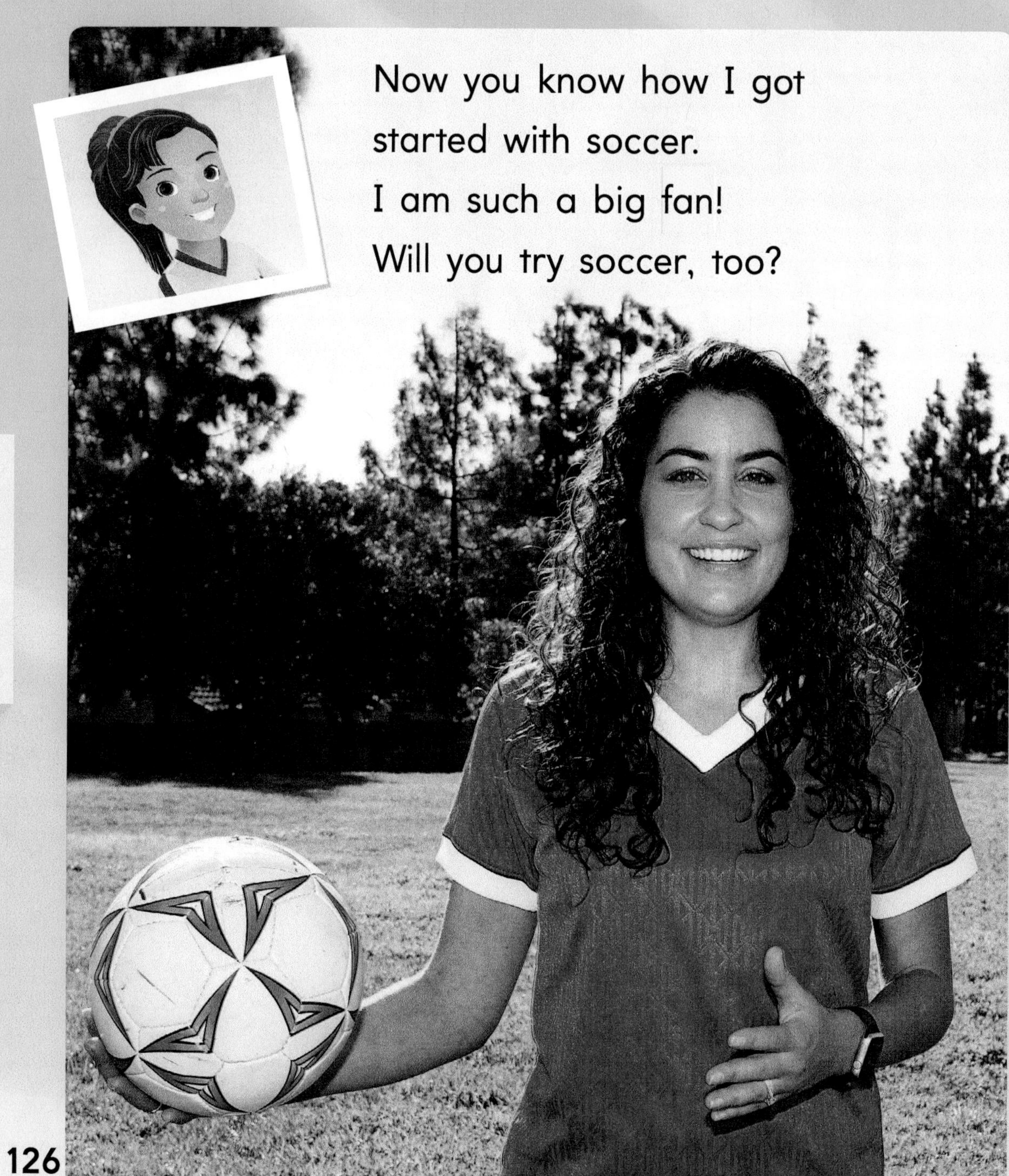

READ FOR UNDERSTANDING

Wrap Up

Revisit the predictions children made before reading. Have them confirm or correct their predictions using evidence from the text and pictures.

DOK 2

Respond to Reading

READ Together

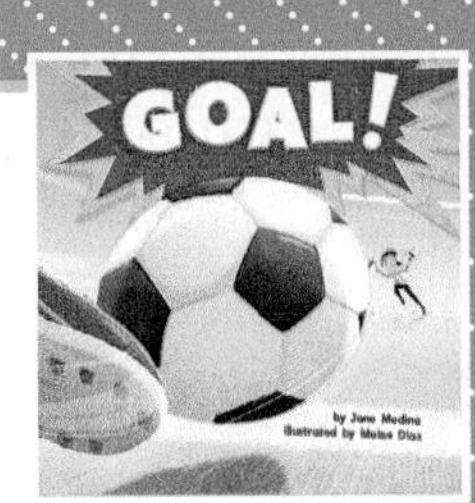

Use details from **Goal!** to answer these questions with a partner.

1. **Evaluate** Which details in **Goal!** are the most important for helping you understand why Colette likes soccer?

2. How do Colette and her team feel when she gets a goal? Why?

Talking Tip

Wait for your turn to talk. Explain your ideas and feelings clearly.

I think that ______________.

Academic Discussion

Use the TURN AND TALK routine. Remind children to listen carefully to their partner, to take turns sharing their ideas, and to explain their ideas and feelings clearly.

Possible responses:

1. *Colette likes to kick and dribble the ball. She is excited to play in her first game. She is excited to get her first goal.* DOK 2
2. *Colette's team feels happy because the team worked together to help Colette score a goal for the team.* DOK 2

Cite Text Evidence

READ Together

Write Game Rules

PROMPT How do you play soccer? Use details from the words and pictures in **Goal!** to explain the rules you learned.

PLAN First, write important words from **Goal!** that tell about playing soccer.

Soccer Words

Write About Reading

- **Read aloud** the prompt.
- **Lead a discussion** in which children recount the rules they learned for playing soccer.
- Then read aloud the Plan section. Have children use ideas from the discussion in their webs.

DOK 3

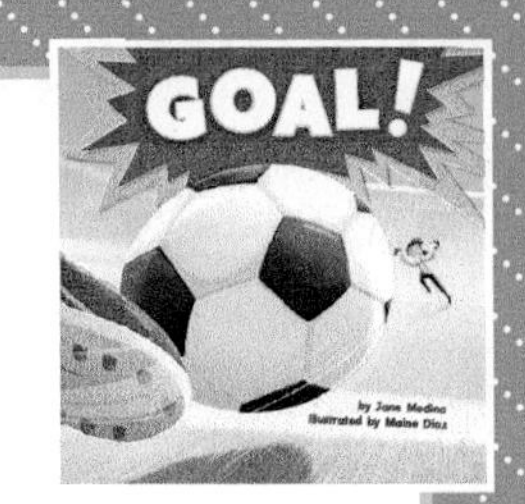

WRITE Now write the rules for playing soccer in your own words. Remember to:

- Use soccer words from your web.
- Use verbs to tell about actions.

Responses may vary.

Write About Reading

- **Read aloud** the Write section.
- **Guide children** to begin each rule with a verb, such as *kick*, *pass*, or *play*.

DOK 3

Independent Close Reading

Have children close read and annotate "Chess Fan" on their own during small-group or independent work time. As needed, **use the Scaffolded Support notes** that follow to guide children who need additional help.

Scaffolded Support

As needed, remind children to:

- evaluate which details are important to the key idea of the text.
- look for clues that help them identify the narrator and determine whether the text is told from a first-person or third-person point of view.

DOK 3

Prepare to Read

GENRE STUDY **Informational text** is nonfiction. It gives facts about a topic.

MAKE A PREDICTION Preview **Chess Fan**. A boy finds out that his school has a chess team. What do you think he will do?

SET A PURPOSE Read to find out if the boy joins the chess team.

Chess Fan

READ What is an important reason to want to play chess?

I am Max. My school has a chess team. Chess looks like a lot of fun. I want to try it! This is how I started to play chess.

Coach sets up the chess game. She tells us all the rules. Meg is my first partner. ▶

Close Reading Tip

Put a ? by the parts you have questions about.

CHECK MY UNDERSTANDING

Who is telling this story? How do you know?

Max. He uses the words I and my.

Scaffolded Support

As needed, guide children to:

- look for words, such as *my*, *me*, and *I* or *he*, *she*, and *they* that can help them figure out who the narrator is.
- ask and answer questions during reading to help them evaluate which details are the most important.

DOK 3

READ What are the most important ideas to remember about playing chess? Underline them.

Close Reading Tip

Write C when you make a connection.

Then we practice. You have to practice to play well. Meg and I play lots of games of chess. Meg is a good partner, and I am, too. We play by the rules. We play fair.

Now I play on the chess team. I play chess every day. I am such a big chess fan!

Scaffolded Support

As needed, remind children to:

- think about each idea and evaluate if it is important to know or remember, or if it is just interesting.
- think about how the children in the selection play fair.
- make connections by finding ways the text is like or unlike something in their lives, in society, or in another text.

DOK 3

CHECK MY UNDERSTANDING

The children are good partners because

they follow the rules and play fair.

Cite Text Evidence

WRITE ABOUT IT What do you need to do to be a good chess player? Write facts you learned from **Chess Fan**. Then share your writing with a partner.

You need to practice a lot to get to be a good chess player. You need to know the rules and play fair.

133

Scaffolded Support

As needed, remind children to reread the text or revisit the important ideas they identified about playing chess.

DOK 2

Guided Practice

Prepare to Read

GENRE STUDY **Informational text** is nonfiction. It gives facts about a topic. Look for:

- headings that stand out
- photographs
- a chart that shows information

POWER WORDS
well
exercise
body

SET A PURPOSE Read to find out the most important ideas in each part. Then **synthesize**, or put the ideas together in your mind, to find out new things about the text and what it really means to you.

Meet Rozanne Lanczak Williams.

134

READ FOR UNDERSTANDING

Introduce the Text

- **Read aloud** and discuss the information about the genre.
- **Guide children** to set a purpose for reading to practice synthesizing important ideas.
- **Provide information** about the author, Rozanne Lanczak Williams.
- **Tell children** to look for and think about the Power Words as they read.

Get UP and GO!

by Rozanne Lanczak Williams

 READ FOR UNDERSTANDING

Make Predictions

- **Page through** the beginning of *Get Up and Go!* with children.
- Have them **use prior knowledge** and what they already know about text organization, headings, special text, and photos to predict what the text will be about. Tell children they will **return to their predictions** after they finish reading the text.

DOK 2

 READ FOR UNDERSTANDING

Concept Words

As children read *Get Up* and *Go!*, they may see familiar words from their speaking and listening vocabularies that they may not know how to read yet. Write these words on the board, read them aloud, and discuss their meanings as needed.

- bikes
- healthy
- hike
- hopscotch
- hour
- muscles
- skate
- stretch
- swim

ASK: **How do you think exercise helps keep you healthy and fit?** *(Possible responses: It makes you strong; it gives you more energy; it makes you feel good.)*

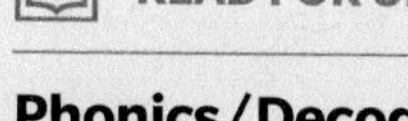

Phonics/Decoding in Context

Have children point to the word *When*. Review that the two letters *wh* stand for one sound, /hw/. **Model blending** the sounds in the word: /hw/ /ĕ/ /n/, *when*. Have children repeat.

Why Exercise?

When you are healthy, you are **well**.

You can get healthy and fit.

How? **Exercise**!

READ FOR UNDERSTANDING

Synthesize

MODEL SYNTHESIZING

THINK ALOUD *When I synthesize, I think about the important things I read in a text and what they mean to me. The important idea I read here is that you need to exercise as much as you can every day. I think about the ways I exercise to stay healthy, such as walking to school. I'll keep this in mind as I read.*

ANNOTATION TIP: Have children underline two ways to get exercise every day.

DOK 3

Exercise with Friends

You could swim and hike with friends. Many kids like bikes.

TARGETED CLOSE READ

Text Features

Have children reread page 138 to analyze text features.

ASK: What information does the heading give you? *(that the text is structured into different parts and this one is about friends exercising together)*

FOLLOW-UP: Why does the author use different color and size text? *(to help readers tell apart the information the character says from the rest of the text)*

ANNOTATION TIP: Have children underline the heading. Then have them circle the rhyming words in the speech balloon.

DOK 3

You could play hopscotch.

You could play fetch with your dog.

Jump and hop.

Play games with Pop.

 **READ FOR UNDERSTANDING**

Synthesize

ASK: What important idea do you learn from pages 138–139? *(that you can exercise with friends by doing things together, like swimming, hiking, biking, or playing games)*

FOLLOW-UP: What does this idea mean to you? *(Possible response: My friends and I do some of these things. I think about other activities we do to get exercise, like playing soccer!)*

DOK 3

 **READ FOR UNDERSTANDING**

Phonics/Decoding in Context

Have children point to the word *with*. Review that the two letters *th* stand for one sound, /th/. **Model blending** the sounds in the word: /th/ /ĭ/ /s/, *this*. Have children repeat.

Word Gaps

- **Remind children** that when an author uses a word or phrase they don't know, they can ask themselves questions to understand the meaning. Explain that understanding important words or phrases can help them synthesize important ideas and think about what the ideas mean to them.
- **Have children** explain how they might use this strategy if they didn't know the phrase *warm up* on page 140. (*I ask myself whether I know this phrase from someplace else. I think about how the phrase is related to exercise. I can also look for clues in the sentences about its meaning.*)

ANNOTATION TIP: Have children underline the phrase *warm up*.

- **Remind them** of the Anchor Question: **Can I find clues in the sentences to help me understand the phrase?** (*The heading "Get Set" and the words "stretch your body" are clues that* warm up *means "to get ready to exercise by stretching."*)

DOK 2

Get Set . . .

It is good to stretch your body. This is a great way to warm up your muscles.

Then you could go for a run.
Just run for fun!
Play tag with your friends.

Jog up a hill.
Then run down.
Jog back,
and jog to town.

READ FOR UNDERSTANDING

Synthesize

MODEL SYNTHESIZING

THINK ALOUD *I think about the important ideas I read on this page. I learn that running is a good way to exercise and that there are different ways to run. I think about what I could do to run more. That seems like an easy way to get exercise!*

DOK 3

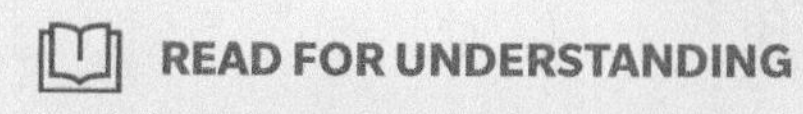

READ FOR UNDERSTANDING

ASK: What kind of team do you play on when you pitch and catch? Kick, toss, or pass? *(Possible responses: baseball, softball; soccer, basketball)*

FOLLOW-UP: What other ways do you exercise when you play these sports? *(Possible responses: run, jump)*

ANNOTATION TIP: Have children underline the action words that name things they do when they play different sports.

DOK 2

Be on a Team

You can find out how to pitch and catch.
You can kick, toss, and pass a ball!

142

Be a Good Sport

Good sports try.
Good sports play fair.
Good sports have fun when they win and when they do not.

Do you know why it is fun to try?

143

 **READ FOR UNDERSTANDING**

Synthesize

ASK: What important idea do you learn from pages 142–143? *(It's important to be a good sport when you play on a team.)*

FOLLOW-UP: What does this mean to you? *(Possible response: When I play on a team, we have more fun when everyone plays fair and is a good sport.)*

DOK 3

It Is Up to You!

How will you get exercise?
Just get up and go!

TARGETED CLOSE READ

Text Features

Have children reread page 144 to analyze text features.

ASK: What does this chart tell you? *(It tells about different kinds of exercise you can try to do.)*

FOLLOW-UP: What do you learn from this chart? *(that everyone can find a way they like to exercise)*

DOK 2

READ FOR UNDERSTANDING

Wrap Up

Revisit the predictions children made before reading. Have them confirm or correct their predictions using evidence from the text and pictures.

DOK 2

If You Like to . . .	You Can Try . . .
 run	  
 jump	  
 kick	  

Respond to Reading

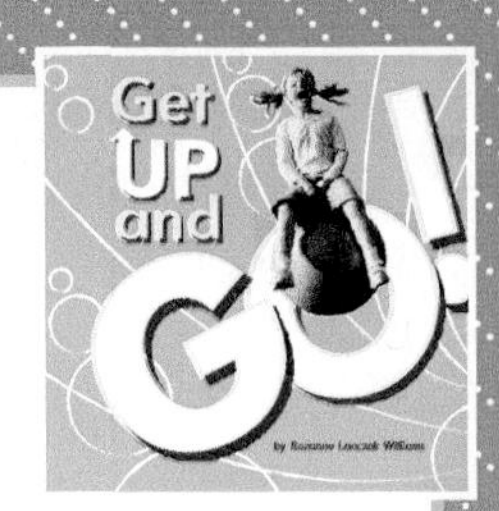

Use details from **Get Up and Go!** to answer these questions with a partner.

1. **Synthesize** What is exercise? Why is exercise important for you?

2. What kinds of exercise can you do on your own? What kinds can you do with others?

Listening Tip

Listen carefully. Think of questions you want to ask your partner when it is your turn to talk.

Academic Discussion

Use the TURN AND TALK routine. Remind children to listen carefully and ask questions about anything they don't understand when it is their turn to speak.

Possible responses:

1. *Exercise is an activity you do to keep your body healthy and well; because I want to stay healthy.* DOK 2
2. *Accept reasonable responses.* DOK 2

Cite Text Evidence

READ Together

Write an Opinion

PROMPT Which way of exercising from **Get Up and Go!** do you think is the best? Use details from the text to help you explain why.

PLAN First, write the kind of exercise you think is best. Write notes about your reasons why.

Reason	Reason	Reason

The best exercise is ______________________________.

146

Write About Reading

- **Read aloud** the prompt.
- **Lead a discussion** in which children recall the different kinds of exercise they read about and say which one they think is best. Tell them to use text evidence to support their ideas.
- Then read aloud the Plan section. Have children use ideas from the discussion in their notes.

DOK 3

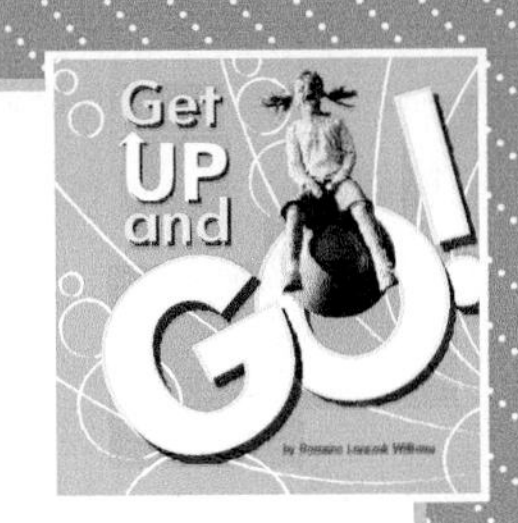

WRITE Now write sentences to tell which way of exercising you think is best. Tell reasons why. Remember to:

- Tell your opinion.
- Use the word **because** when you write a reason.

Responses may vary.

Write About Reading

- **Read aloud** the Write section.
- **Guide children** to state their opinions clearly and to include their reasons, using the word *because*.

DOK 3

Independent Close Reading

Have children close read and annotate "Play Tag!" on their own during small-group or independent work time. As needed, **use the Scaffolded Support notes** that follow to guide children who need additional help.

Scaffolded Support

As needed, remind children to:

- synthesize information in a text by identifying the important ideas as they read and thinking about what those ideas mean to them.
- look for text and graphic features, such as bold text, different color text, and headings that help them understand information.

DOK 3

On My Own

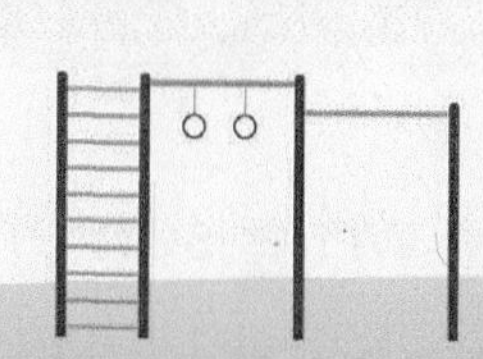

Prepare to Read

GENRE STUDY **Informational text** is nonfiction. It gives facts about a topic.

MAKE A PREDICTION Preview **Play Tag!** Use the title, headings, pictures, and chart to help you predict. What do you think you will learn?

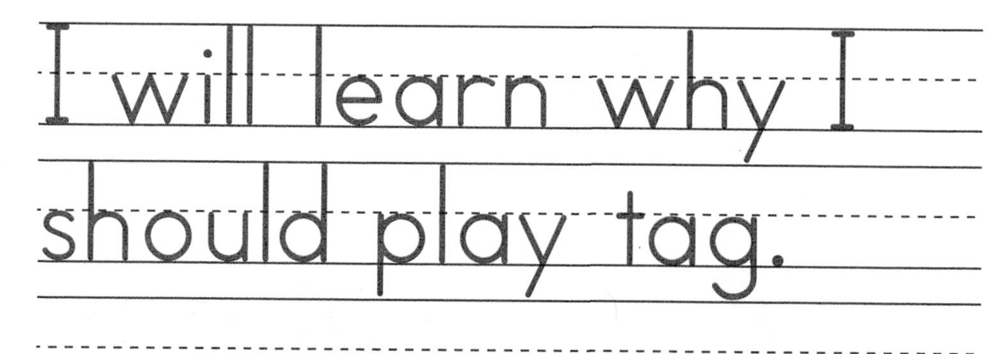

SET A PURPOSE Read to find out how and why to play tag.

Play Tag!

READ Why is the title big? Why are some words red? What do the red words tell you about this part?

Rules for Tag

Tag is a fun game that friends can play together. Pick one friend to be It. Then everyone runs. The friend who is It runs, too. If the friend who is It can catch you, then you are the new It! ▶

Close Reading Tip
Write C when you make a connection.

CHECK MY UNDERSTANDING

Why is the player who is It important in tag?

It tags someone. That person is the new It.

Scaffolded Support

As needed, remind children that:

- headings, which are usually bigger and sometimes a different color than the rest of the text, help organize the information by topic.
- they can reread the text and think about which ideas are most important about the player called It.

DOK 3

READ What are the two parts of the chart? What do you learn about tag from each part?

How Tag Helps You

Do you know how to be healthy? Play tag!

Helps Your Body	Helps You Be Happy
It is good exercise.	Tag is fun.
You run a lot.	A fun game makes you happy.
It is good for your muscles.	Many friends can play together.

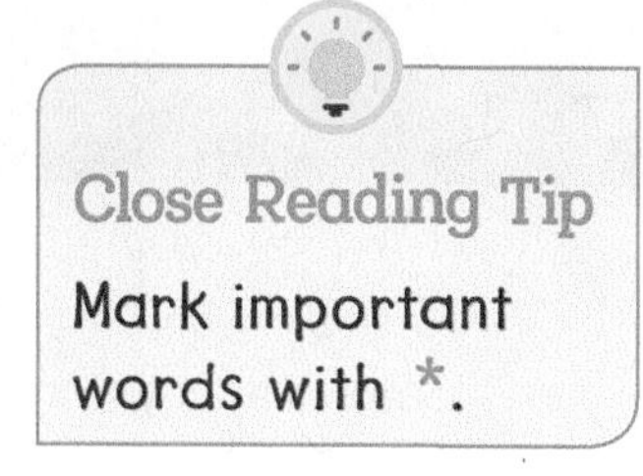

Close Reading Tip

Mark important words with *.

Scaffolded Support

As needed, remind children to:

- think about why the author chose to include the chart and what information it gives.
- identify each idea and think about which ones are most important for understanding the game of tag.

DOK 2

CHECK MY UNDERSTANDING

What important things did you learn about tag?

It is a fun game to play with friends. It helps you be healthy.

Cite Text Evidence

WRITE ABOUT IT After reading **Play Tag!**, how do you feel about the game? Write sentences to tell what playing tag means to you. Use ideas from **Play Tag!** to give reasons for why you think as you do. Share your writing with classmates.

I think tag is one of the best games to play. It is good exercise. I think it's fun to tag my friends. I like to run, so I like tag!

151

Scaffolded Support

As needed, guide children to:

- form an opinion about the game of tag based on what they read and their own experiences playing tag.
- include reasons for their opinions in their writing.
- share their writing with their classmates.

DOK 2

 READ FOR UNDERSTANDING

Introduce the Text

- **Read aloud** and discuss the information about the genre.
- **Guide children** to set a purpose for reading to practice retelling story events in order.
- **Provide information** about the author and illustrator, Mo Willems.
- **Tell children** to look for and think about the Power Words as they read.

Prepare to Read

GENRE STUDY **Fantasy** stories have made-up events that could not really happen. Look for:

- animals that talk and act like people
- ways the pictures help you understand
- a problem and resolution

SET A PURPOSE Read to understand events in the beginning, middle, and end. Look for details in the words and pictures to help you. **Retell** the events in your own words.

POWER WORDS
guy
hero
excuse

Meet Mo Willems.

152

A Big Guy Took My Ball!

by Mo Willems

 READ FOR UNDERSTANDING

Make Predictions

- **Page through** the beginning of *A Big Guy Took My Ball!* with children.
- Have them **use prior knowledge** and the text and graphic features, including the illustrations and the dialogue in the speech balloons, to predict what the story will be about. Tell children they will **return to their predictions** after they finish reading the story.

DOK 2

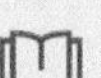 READ FOR UNDERSTANDING

Concept Words

As children read *A Big Guy Took My Ball!*, they may see familiar words from their speaking and listening vocabularies that they may not know how to read yet. Write these words on the board, read them aloud, and discuss their meanings as needed.

- bigger
- biggy-big-big
- size
- smaller

READ FOR UNDERSTANDING

ASK: Who is talking? *(Piggie)*

FOLLOW-UP: How can you tell? *(The author shows her words in speech balloons that point from her.)*

DOK 2

154

And then a big guy came—

and—

and—

and—

155

READ FOR UNDERSTANDING

ANNOTATION TIP: Have children circle the repeated words on this page.

ASK: Why do you think the author repeated these words? *(Possible response: to build excitement about what happens)*

FOLLOW-UP: What mental image do these words help you make? *(Possible response: The sound of Piggie stammering because she is very upset.)*

DOK 2

HE TOOK

READ FOR UNDERSTANDING

ASK: What is Piggie's problem and how does she feel about it? *(A big guy took her ball; she is very upset.)*

FOLLOW-UP: How do you know? *(Piggie's words are shown in big text to show that she is shouting. The picture shows her crying, and Gerald being knocked over by her loud words.)*

DOK 2

156

MY BALL!

157

 READ FOR UNDERSTANDING

Retell

MODEL RETELLING

THINK ALOUD *Retelling a story can help me understand it. When I retell a story, I use my own words to tell what happens. At the beginning of this story, Piggie tells her friend about how much fun she was having with a big ball she found. But then a big guy took the ball!*

DOK 2

TARGETED CLOSE READ

Characters

Have children reread pages 158–163 to identify and describe the characters.

ASK: What do you know about the characters? *(Piggie, a small pig, and Gerald, a big elephant, are friends.)*

FOLLOW-UP: Why does Gerald go get Piggie's ball? *(Possible response: because he cares about Piggie and wants her to feel better)*

DOK 2

158

159

READ FOR UNDERSTANDING

ASK: **How does Gerald react when he finds out what happened?** *(First he is surprised, then sad, and then he gets mad.)*

ANNOTATION TIP: Have children write a describing word next to each picture of Gerald that tells how he feels.

DOK 2

160

READ FOR UNDERSTANDING

Phonics/Decoding in Context

Have children point to the word *guys*. Review that the ending *-s* can change the word to mean more than one. **Model blending** the sounds in the word: /g/ /ī/ /z/, *guys*. Have children repeat.

ANNOTATION TIP: Have children circle the *-s* at the end of *guys*.

161

READ FOR UNDERSTANDING

ASK: What do the pictures tell you about how Piggie is feeling on pages 160–161? *(They show she is surprised and confused about what Gerald is saying.)*

FOLLOW-UP: What does the text say about how Piggie is feeling? *(Possible response: She asks Gerald a question because she is confused.)*

DOK 2

READ FOR UNDERSTANDING

Phonics/Decoding in Context

Have children point to the word *makes*. Review that the ending *-s* can change the meaning of action words. Model blending the sounds in the word: /m/ /ā/ /k//s/, *makes*. Have children repeat.

ANNOTATION TIP: Have children circle the *-s* at the end of *makes*.

WELL, I AM *BIG* TOO!

162

 **READ FOR UNDERSTANDING**

ASK: Why does the author show Gerald's words in capital letters? *(to show that Gerald is shouting)*

FOLLOW-UP: What other details help you understand this? *(The picture shows Gerald with his mouth wide open and Piggie shrinking down because of the noise.)*

DOK 2

I will get your big ball from that big guy!

163

READ FOR UNDERSTANDING

Retell

MODEL RETELLING

THINK ALOUD *I will pause here to check that I understand what is happening by retelling in my own words. The elephant, Gerald, gets very upset. He thinks that a big guy took Piggie's ball just because he was bigger than Piggie. He decides he is going to get the ball back.*

DOK 2

READ FOR UNDERSTANDING

ASK: How does Piggie feel when Gerald goes to get the ball?
(She's happy.)

FOLLOW-UP: How do you know?
(She is smiling and thinking that Gerald is her hero.)

DOK 2

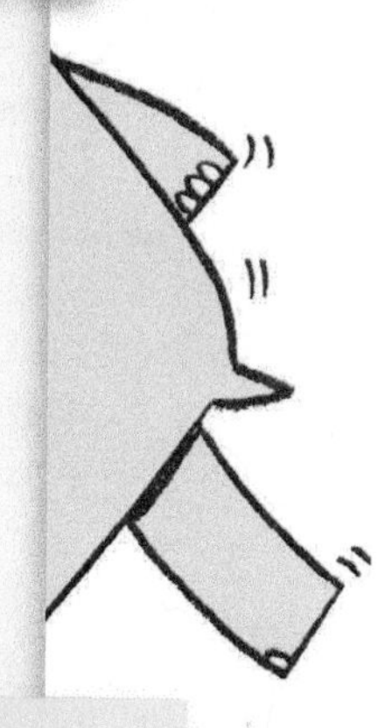

READ FOR UNDERSTANDING

ASK: What picture do you make in your mind about the big guy?
(Accept reasonable responses.)

DOK 2

164

165

READ FOR UNDERSTANDING

ASK: What kind of friend is Gerald? *(Possible responses: a good friend; a helpful friend)*

FOLLOW-UP: What evidence tells you this? *(He listens carefully to Piggie; he wants to help Piggie.)*

DOK 2

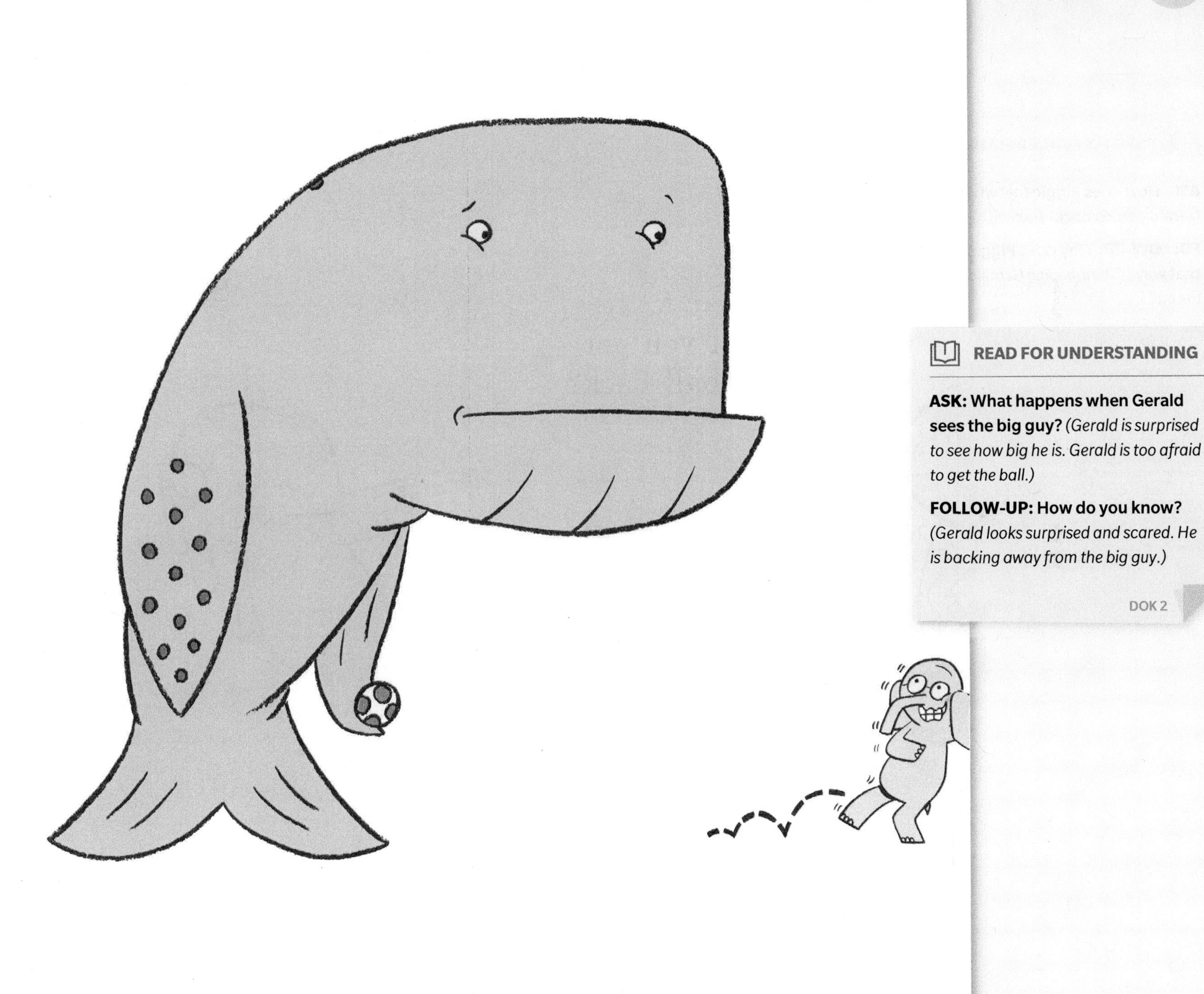

READ FOR UNDERSTANDING

ASK: What happens when Gerald sees the big guy? *(Gerald is surprised to see how big he is. Gerald is too afraid to get the ball.)*

FOLLOW-UP: How do you know? *(Gerald looks surprised and scared. He is backing away from the big guy.)*

DOK 2

READ FOR UNDERSTANDING

ASK: How does Piggie feel when Gerald comes back? *(excited)*

FOLLOW-UP: Why does Piggie feel that way? *(She is hoping Gerald got the ball.)*

DOK 2

168

You did not say *how* big he was.

He is very

BIG

READ FOR UNDERSTANDING

ANNOTATION TIP: Have children circle the repeated word on pages 168–169.

ASK: Why does Gerald keep repeating the word *big*? *(He's still surprised at how big the big guy is.)*

DOK 2

READ FOR UNDERSTANDING

ASK: Why doesn't Gerald answer Piggie's question? *(Possible response: He doesn't want to admit that he was too scared to get the ball.)*

DOK 2

170

171

READ FOR UNDERSTANDING

Retell

ASK: What happens in this part of the story? *(Gerald goes to get the ball back, but sees that the big guy is MUCH bigger than him. He is afraid of him and does not even try to get the ball back.)*

DOK 2

EXCUSE

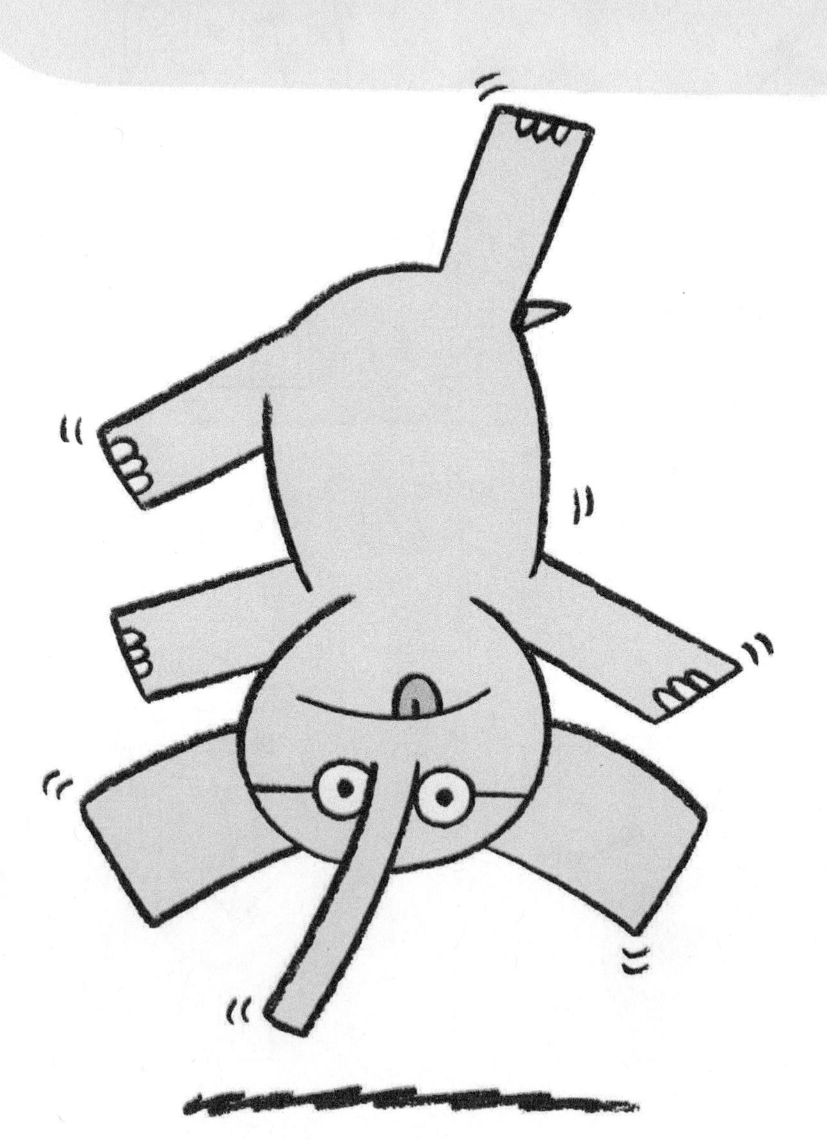

ME!

173

READ FOR UNDERSTANDING

ASK: Who is talking now? *(the big guy)*

FOLLOW-UP: Why do you think that? *(Possible responses: because the big guy saw Gerald; the words are shown in very big letters, which could mean that someone who is very big is talking.)*

DOK 2

TARGETED CLOSE READ

Characters

Have children reread pages 174–180 to analyze the story characters.

ASK: Why do Gerald and Piggie ask the buy guy to play? *(They are being nice.)*

FOLLOW-UP: How do you know? *(The words say that no one wants to play with the big guy and the pictures show that Gerald and Piggie feel bad about it.)*

DOK 2

THANK YOU FOR FINDING MY LITTLE BALL.

174

That is *your* ball?

And you think it is little?

READ FOR UNDERSTANDING

ASK: What do Piggie and Gerald learn? *(that the ball belongs to the big guy)*

FOLLOW-UP: Why is Piggie surprised that the big guy thinks the ball is little? *(because it is big compared to her)*

DOK 2

WELL,
I AM
BIG.

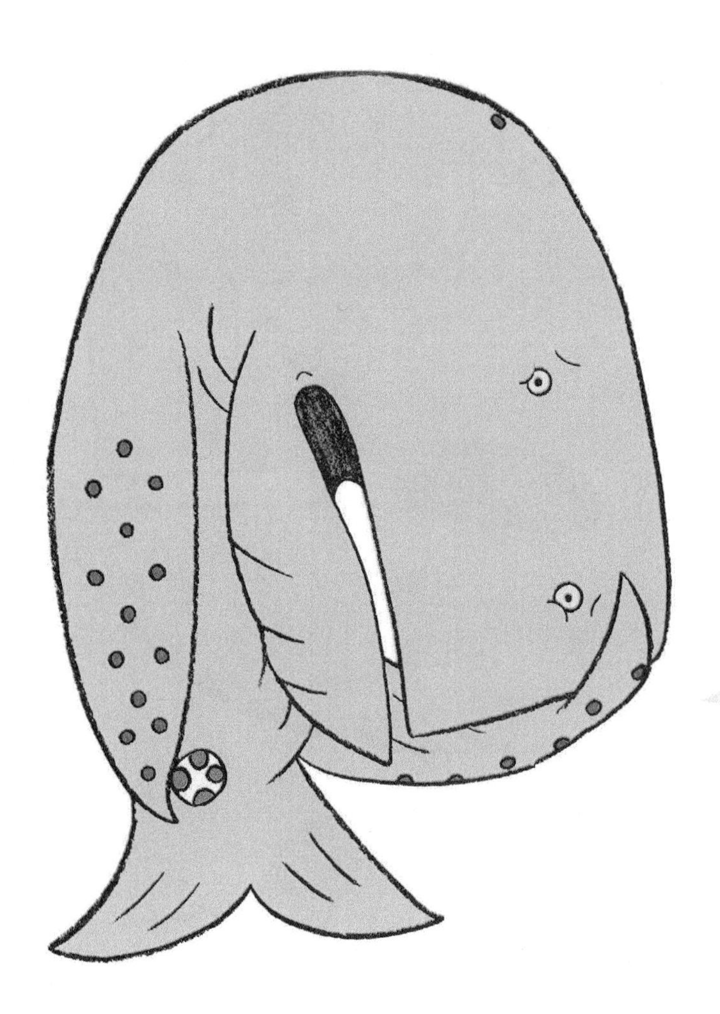

SO BIG THAT NO ONE WILL PLAY WITH ME.

READ FOR UNDERSTANDING

ASK: What is Big Guy's problem? *(No one will play with him because he is so big.)*

FOLLOW-UP: What do Piggie and Gerald think about this? *(They are very surprised.)*

ANNOTATION TIP: Have children label the characters with a word that describes how each character feels.

DOK 2

READ FOR UNDERSTANDING

ASK: What do you think Gerald and Piggie will do? *(Possible response: They might play with the big guy.)*

DOK 2

LITTLE GUYS HAVE
ALL THE FUN.

179

Notice & Note

Aha Moment

- **Remind children** that when they are reading and a character realizes something, they should stop to notice and note. Explain that retelling what has happened so far can help them think about how the story might change.
- **Have children** tell how this strategy can help them on pages 178–179. *(When Piggie and Gerald finally talk to the big guy, they realize that he is not mean.)*

ANNOTATION TIP: Have children circle the details in the picture that help them understand that Piggie and Gerald have changed their minds about the big guy.

- **Remind children** of the Anchor Question: **How might this change things?** *(Now that Gerald and Piggie realize how the big guy feels, they might be friendly to him.)*

DOK 3

READ FOR UNDERSTANDING

ASK: What idea do Gerald and Piggie have? *(that they all play together)*

FOLLOW-UP: How does this solve Piggie's and Big Guy's problems? *(Piggie can play with the ball and Big Guy can have fun with his new friends.)*

DOK 2

180

181

READ FOR UNDERSTANDING

ASK: Why do you think Piggie and Gerald suggest a made-up game? *(They want to do something that will be fun for everyone.)*

DOK 2

 READ FOR UNDERSTANDING

Retell

ASK: What happens at the end of the story? *(The big guy comes and thanks Gerald and Piggie for finding his ball. He is sad that no one will play with him because he is so big. Piggie and Gerald realize they were wrong about him and ask him to play a new game with them. They all have fun.)*

DOK 2

 READ FOR UNDERSTANDING

Wrap Up

Revisit the predictions children made before reading. Have them confirm or correct their predictions using evidence from the text and pictures.

DOK 2

182

Respond to Reading

READ Together

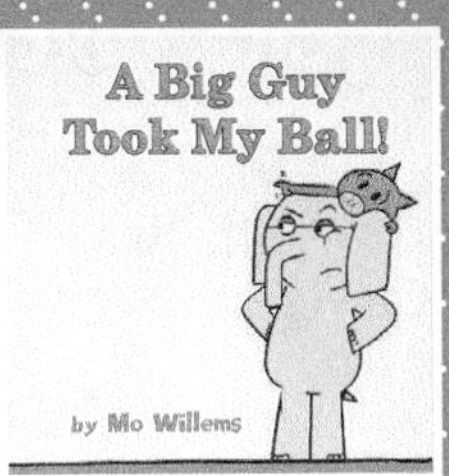

Use details from **A Big Guy Took My Ball!** to answer these questions with a partner.

1. **Retell** Tell the story in your own words. Tell about the main events that happen in the beginning, middle, and end.

2. How do Gerald's ideas about big guys change during the story?

Talking Tip

Speak clearly. Do not speak too fast or too slow.

My idea is ______________.

Academic Discussion

Use the TURN AND TALK routine. Remind children to speak clearly at a speed that is not too fast and not too slow.

Possible responses:

1. *At the beginning, Piggie found a ball, but a big guy took it. In the middle, Gerald went to get the ball back, but the guy was so big that Gerald was scared. Then the big guy came to thank them for finding his ball. Gerald and Piggie found out the big guy wasn't mean and had no one to play with. So, at the end, they came up with a new game that they can all play together.* DOK 2
2. *At first, Gerald thinks all big guys are mean and have all the fun, but then he finds out that big guys can be lonely because no one wants to play with them.* DOK 2

Cite Text Evidence

READ Together

Write Game Directions

PROMPT How will the characters in **A Big Guy Took My Ball!** play "Whale Ball"? Write directions for the game. Use the story for ideas.

PLAN First, write or draw what to do to play "Whale Ball." Add numbers to show the order of the steps.

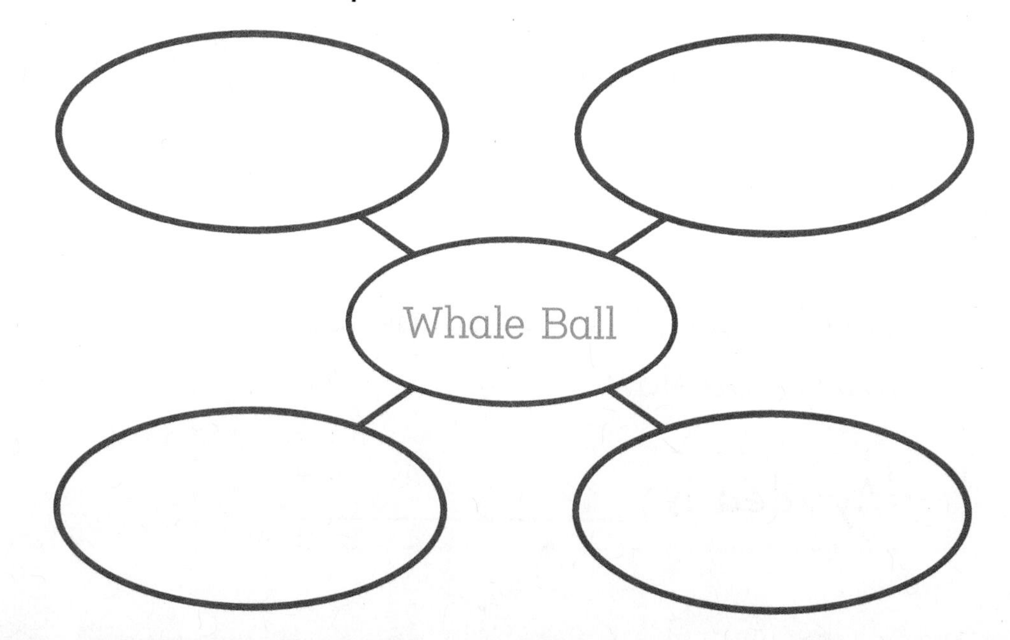

Write About Reading

- **Read aloud** the prompt.
- **Lead a discussion** in which children describe different ways the characters could play "Whale Ball." Tell them to use text evidence to support their ideas.
- Then read aloud the Plan section. Have children use ideas from the discussion in their directions, adding numbers to show the order of the steps.

DOK 3

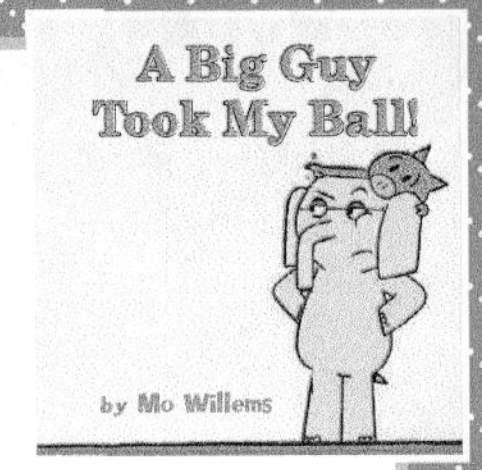

WRITE Now write the directions for how to play "Whale Ball." Remember to:

- Write the steps in order.
- Use verbs to tell about actions.

Responses may vary.

185

Write About Reading

- **Read aloud** the Write section.
- **Encourage children** to retell their directions to make sure they have written the steps in an order that makes sense, and that they include action words.

DOK 3

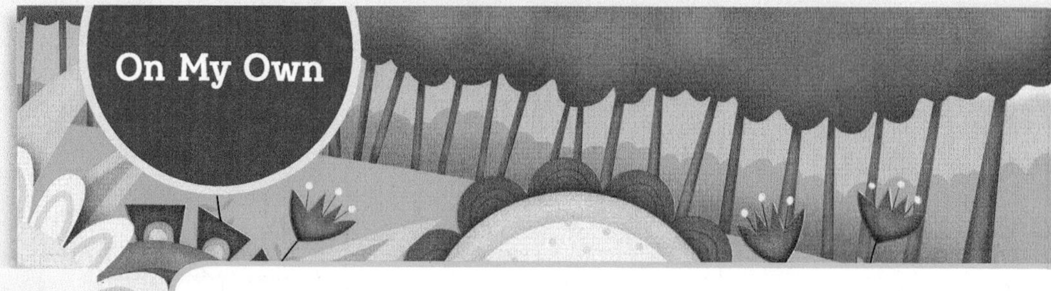

Independent Close Reading

Have children close read and annotate "Biggy-Big-Big!" on their own during small-group or independent work time. As needed, **use the Scaffolded Support notes** that follow to guide children who need additional help.

Scaffolded Support

As needed, remind children to:

- pause and retell what happens in the story to help them understand and remember what they are reading.
- use clues in the text and illustrations to help them describe the characters and understand why they do what they do.

DOK 2

Prepare to Read

GENRE STUDY **Fantasy** stories have made-up events that could not really happen.

MAKE A PREDICTION Preview **Biggy-Big-Big!** Fox is always bragging about how big he is. What do you think will happen?

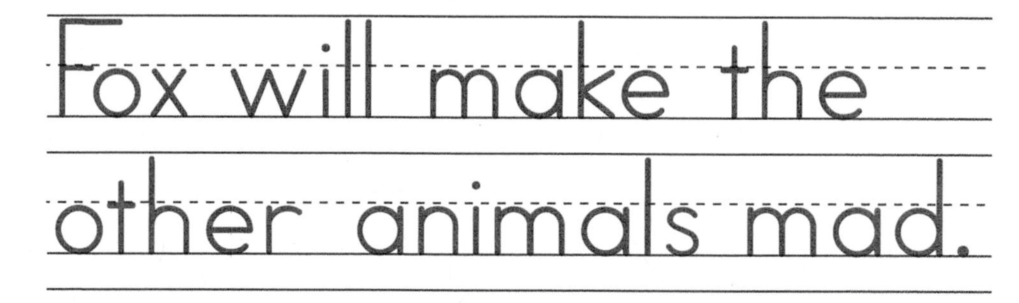

SET A PURPOSE Read to find out what Fox does and what happens. Find out if your prediction is right.

Biggy-Big-Big!

READ Underline the names of the characters. Describe them.

"Look at me!" said Fox. "See how great I am? I am bigger than you, Duck. I am bigger than you, Bug. I am bigger than everyone. I am biggy-big-big!" Fox would not play with Duck and Bug. It made them sad. ▶

CHECK MY UNDERSTANDING

Why do you think Fox acts the way he does?

He thinks he is better because he is bigger.

187

Scaffolded Support

As needed, guide children to:

- look for words that name the people, animals, or things the story is about.
- look for words that tell what Fox says and does.
- think about why Fox does what he does.
- think about what happens first, next, and last to help them number the events.

DOK 2

READ What is Baby Yak like? Underline words that tell.

Just then, Baby Yak ran by. She saw Duck and Bug. "Will you play with me?" Baby Yak asked them in a kind way.

Duck said, "Look, Fox! Baby Yak will play with us. And she is much bigger than you."

Fox saw that Baby Yak was BIGGY-BIG-BIG! He said, "I am very sorry, Duck and Bug."

Close Reading Tip

Put a ? by the parts you have questions about.

Scaffolded Support

As needed, remind children that:

- details in the words and pictures can help them understand what the characters are like throughout the story.
- asking and answering questions as they read will help them make sure they understand what is happening in the story.

DOK 2

CHECK MY UNDERSTANDING

How does Fox change by the end of the story?

Fox stops bragging. He is nicer and says he is sorry.

Cite Text Evidence

DRAW IT Draw a picture of what you think the animals do after Fox says he is sorry. Add a caption to tell about it. Then tell the whole story **Biggy-Big-Big!** to a partner. Tell the main events that happen in the beginning, middle, and end.

Fox, Duck, Bug, and Baby Yak play tag.

189

Scaffolded Support

As needed, guide children to use what they know about the characters to help them draw a picture and write a caption to describe what happens next in the story. Remind them to retell story events in order.

DOK 3

READ FOR UNDERSTANDING

Introduce the Text

- **Read aloud** and discuss the information about the genre.
- **Guide children** to set a purpose for reading to practice making connections.
- **Provide information** about the author and illustrator, Kadir Nelson.
- **Tell children** to look for and think about the Power Words as they read.

Guided Practice

Prepare to Read

GENRE STUDY **Fantasy** stories have made-up events that could not really happen. Look for:

- animals that act like people
- a lesson the characters learn
- ways pictures help you understand

SET A PURPOSE As you read, **make connections** by finding ways that this text is like things in your life and other texts you have read. This will help you understand and remember the text.

POWER WORDS
seed
short
heap
trouble
fruits

Meet Kadir Nelson.

190

If You Plant a Seed

by Kadir Nelson

READ FOR UNDERSTANDING

Make Predictions

- **Page through** the beginning of *If You Plant a Seed* with children.
- Have them **use prior knowledge** and the illustrations to predict what the story will be about. Tell children they will **return to their predictions** after they finish reading the story.

DOK 2

READ FOR UNDERSTANDING

Concept Words

As children read *If You Plant a Seed,* they may see familiar words from their speaking and listening vocabularies that they may not know how to read yet. Write these words on the board, read them aloud, and discuss their meanings as needed.

- cabbage
- carrot
- plant
- tomato

If you plant a tomato seed,

a carrot seed,

and a cabbage seed,

192

READ FOR UNDERSTANDING

ASK: What are the rabbit and the mouse doing? *(They are planting seeds.)*

FOLLOW-UP: What evidence tells you this? *(The picture shows a rabbit and a mouse dropping a seed into the ground; the text tells which seeds they are planting.)*

ANNOTATION TIP: Have children underline the words that name the kinds of seeds the rabbit and the mouse plant.

DOK 2

in time,

READ FOR UNDERSTANDING

ASK: How long does it take for the seeds to begin to grow? *(many days and nights)*

FOLLOW-UP: How do you know? *(The text says "in time." The pictures show different days and nights.)*

ANNOTATION TIP: Have children underline the phrase in the text that tells them time has passed.

DOK 2

READ FOR UNDERSTANDING

ASK: How do the characters feel about taking care of the seeds? *(They like it at the beginning but then they get tired.)*

FOLLOW-UP: How do you know? *(The pictures show them doing different things at first, but then they get wet and fall asleep.)*

DOK 2

with love and care,

194

tomato,

carrot,

and cabbage

plants will grow.

195

READ FOR UNDERSTANDING

ASK: Why are the rabbit and the mouse hopping up and down? *(They are happy that their vegetables have grown.)*

ANNOTATION TIP: Have children draw a line from each vegetable to the word that names it.

DOK 2

READ FOR UNDERSTANDING

Make Connections

MODEL MAKING A CONNECTION

THINK ALOUD *The rabbit and the mouse plant vegetable seeds and are excited when they grow. This reminds me of our community garden. People plant all kinds of vegetables there. It takes a long time, but everyone is very excited when the plants grow!*

DOK 3

197

READ FOR UNDERSTANDING

ASK: What is happening on these pages? *(The rabbit and the mouse notice that the birds are staring at them; the birds look like they want some of the vegetables.)*

DOK 2

TARGETED CLOSE READ

Theme

Have children reread pages 198–201 to analyze the theme of the story.

ASK: Why are the animals fighting? *(The rabbit and mouse don't share with the birds.)*

FOLLOW-UP: What is this part of the story mostly about? *(what happens when you are not kind to others)*

DOK 3

READ FOR UNDERSTANDING

Quick Teach Words

As needed to support comprehension, briefly explain the meaning of the word *selfishness*.

- If you act with *selfishness*, you only think about yourself and not about the feelings or needs of others.

198

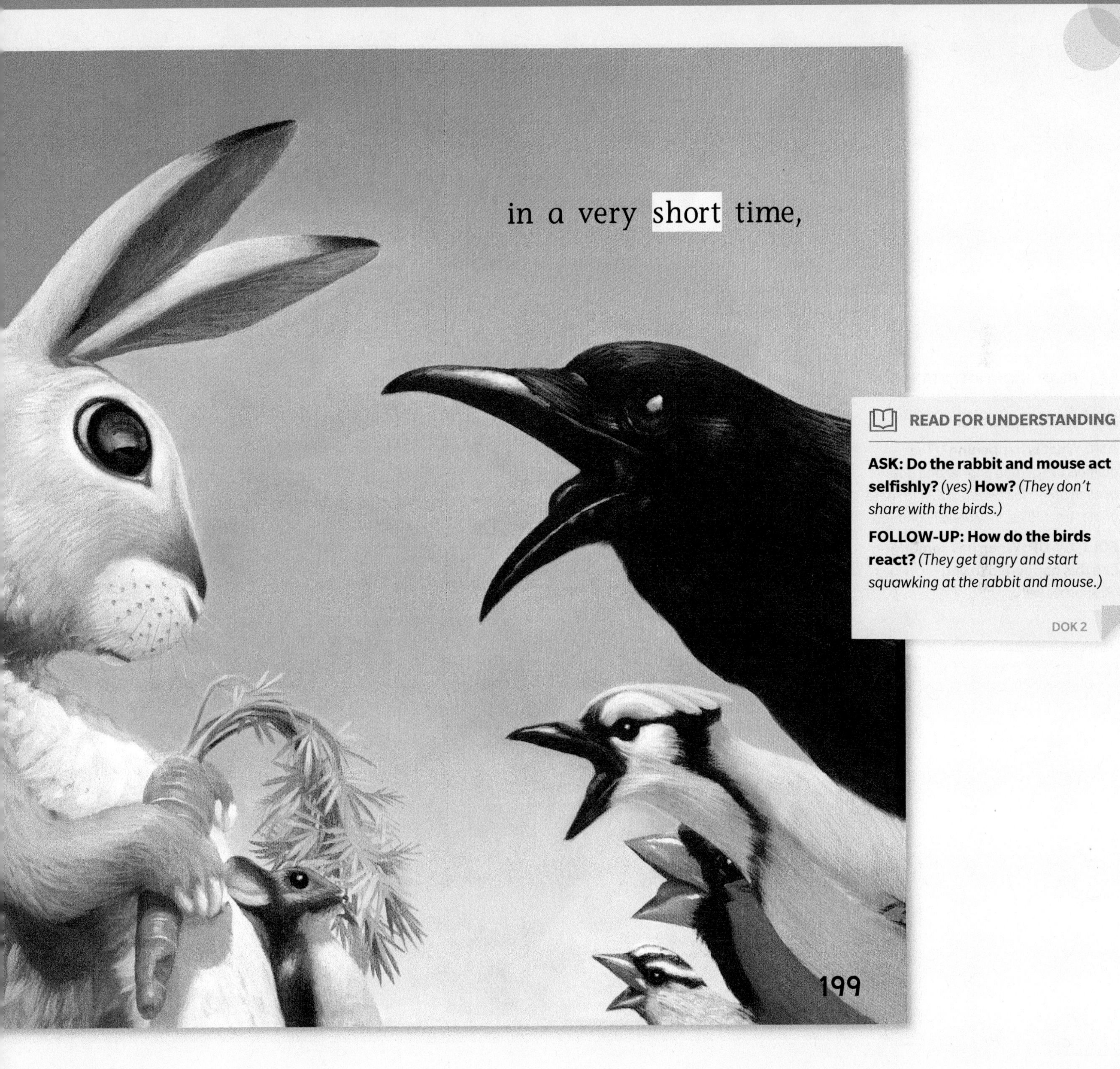

in a very short time,

199

READ FOR UNDERSTANDING

ASK: Do the rabbit and mouse act selfishly? *(yes)* **How?** *(They don't share with the birds.)*

FOLLOW-UP: How do the birds react? *(They get angry and start squawking at the rabbit and mouse.)*

DOK 2

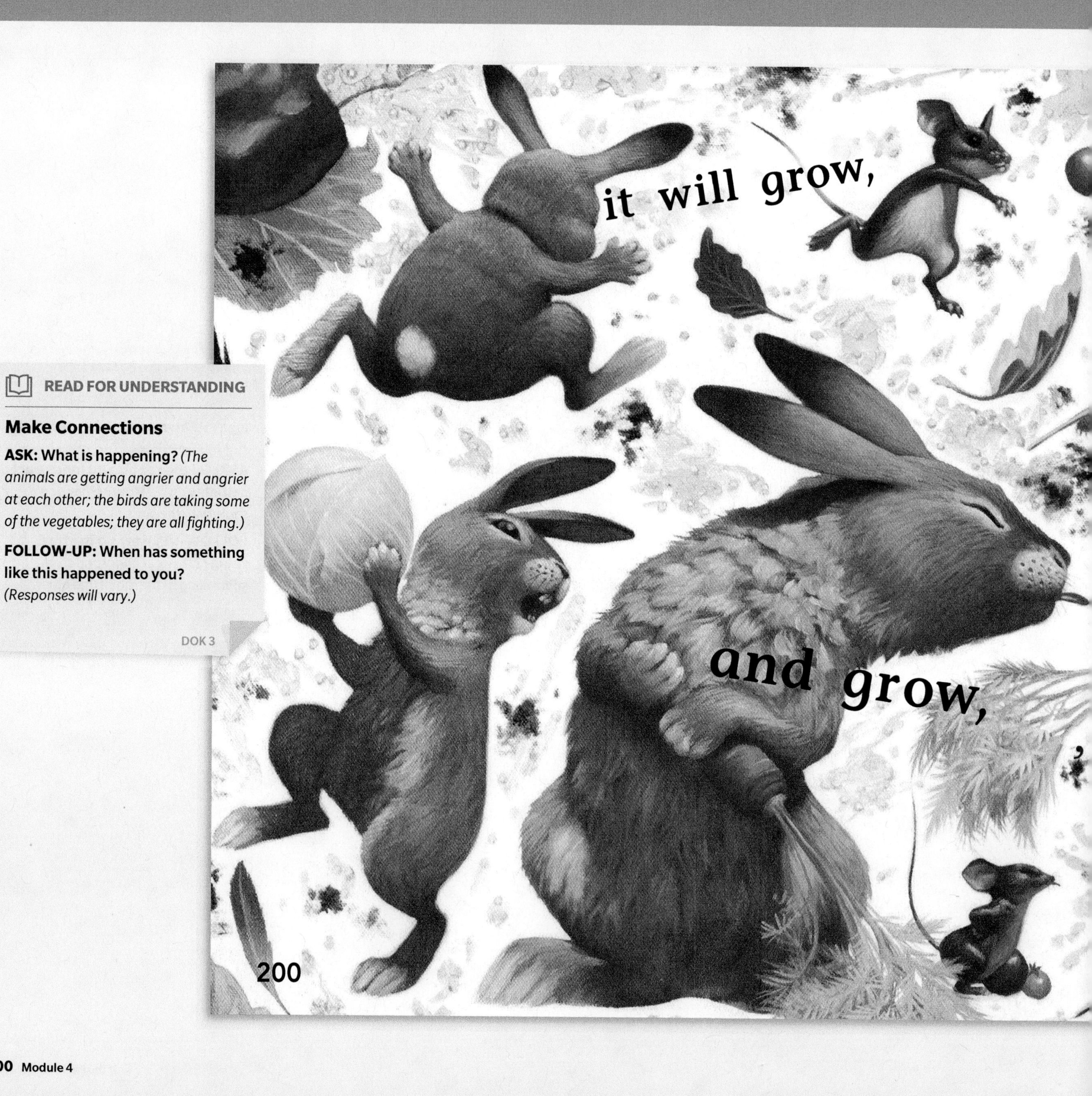

READ FOR UNDERSTANDING

Make Connections

ASK: **What is happening?** *(The animals are getting angrier and angrier at each other; the birds are taking some of the vegetables; they are all fighting.)*

FOLLOW-UP: **When has something like this happened to you?** *(Responses will vary.)*

DOK 3

READ FOR UNDERSTANDING

ASK: Why does the author repeat the word *grow*? *(to let the reader know that the bad feelings get worse and worse)*

ANNOTATION TIP: Have children circle the repeated word.

FOLLOW-UP: What else does the author do to draw attention to this idea? *(He makes the size of the text get bigger and bigger.)*

DOK 2

Notice & Note

Aha Moment

- **Remind children** that when they are reading and a character realizes something, they should stop to notice and note. Explain that making connections to what is happening can help them think about how the story might change.
- **Have children** tell how this strategy can help them on page 202. *(The mouse and the rabbit realize that being selfish made a mess of the garden and made everyone unhappy.)*
- **Remind children** of the Anchor Question: **How might this change things?** *(The animals will share and be kind to each other.)*

DOK 3

into a heap

of trouble.

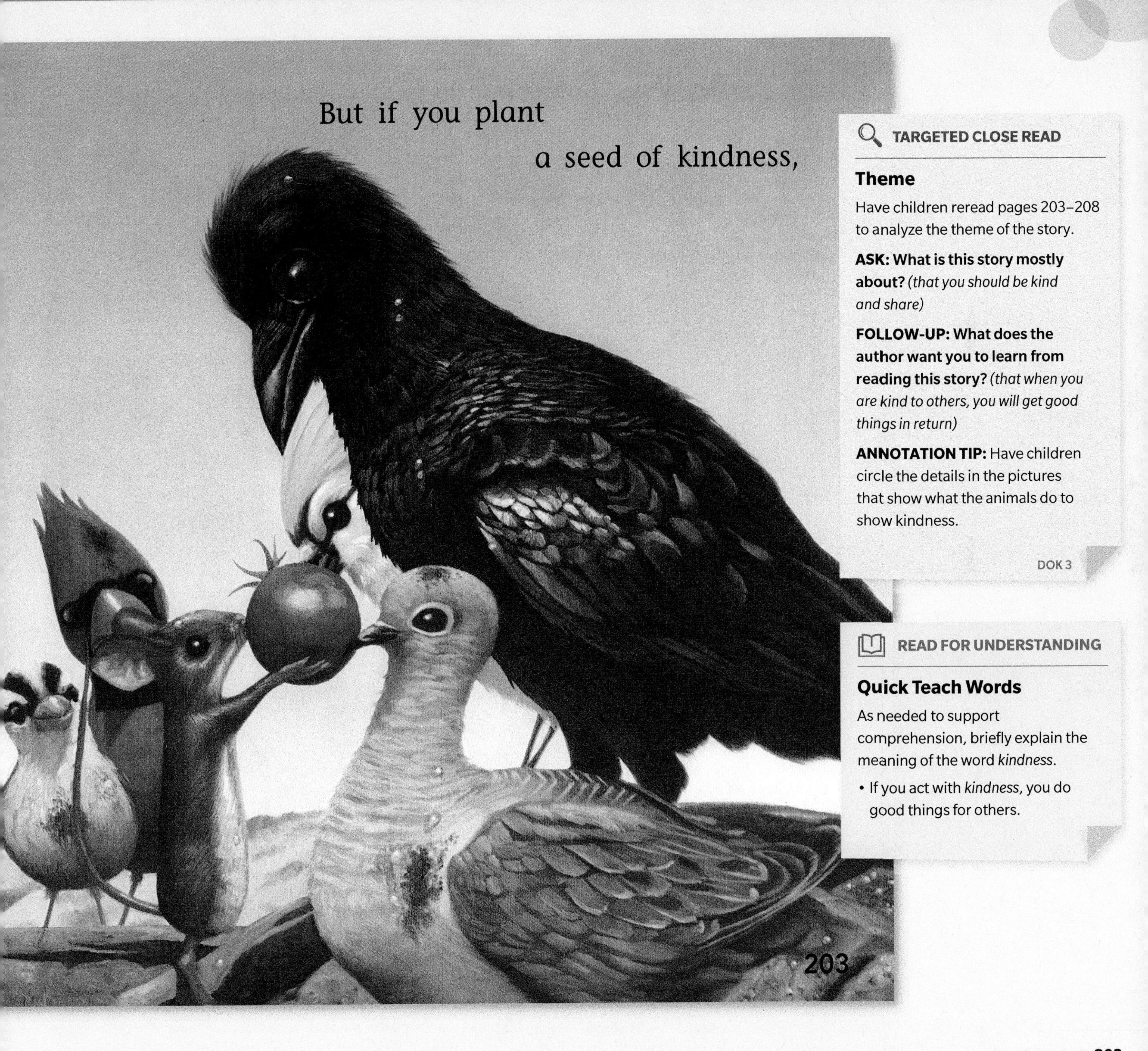

TARGETED CLOSE READ

Theme

Have children reread pages 203–208 to analyze the theme of the story.

ASK: What is this story mostly about? *(that you should be kind and share)*

FOLLOW-UP: What does the author want you to learn from reading this story? *(that when you are kind to others, you will get good things in return)*

ANNOTATION TIP: Have children circle the details in the pictures that show what the animals do to show kindness.

DOK 3

READ FOR UNDERSTANDING

Quick Teach Words

As needed to support comprehension, briefly explain the meaning of the word *kindness*.

- If you act with *kindness*, you do good things for others.

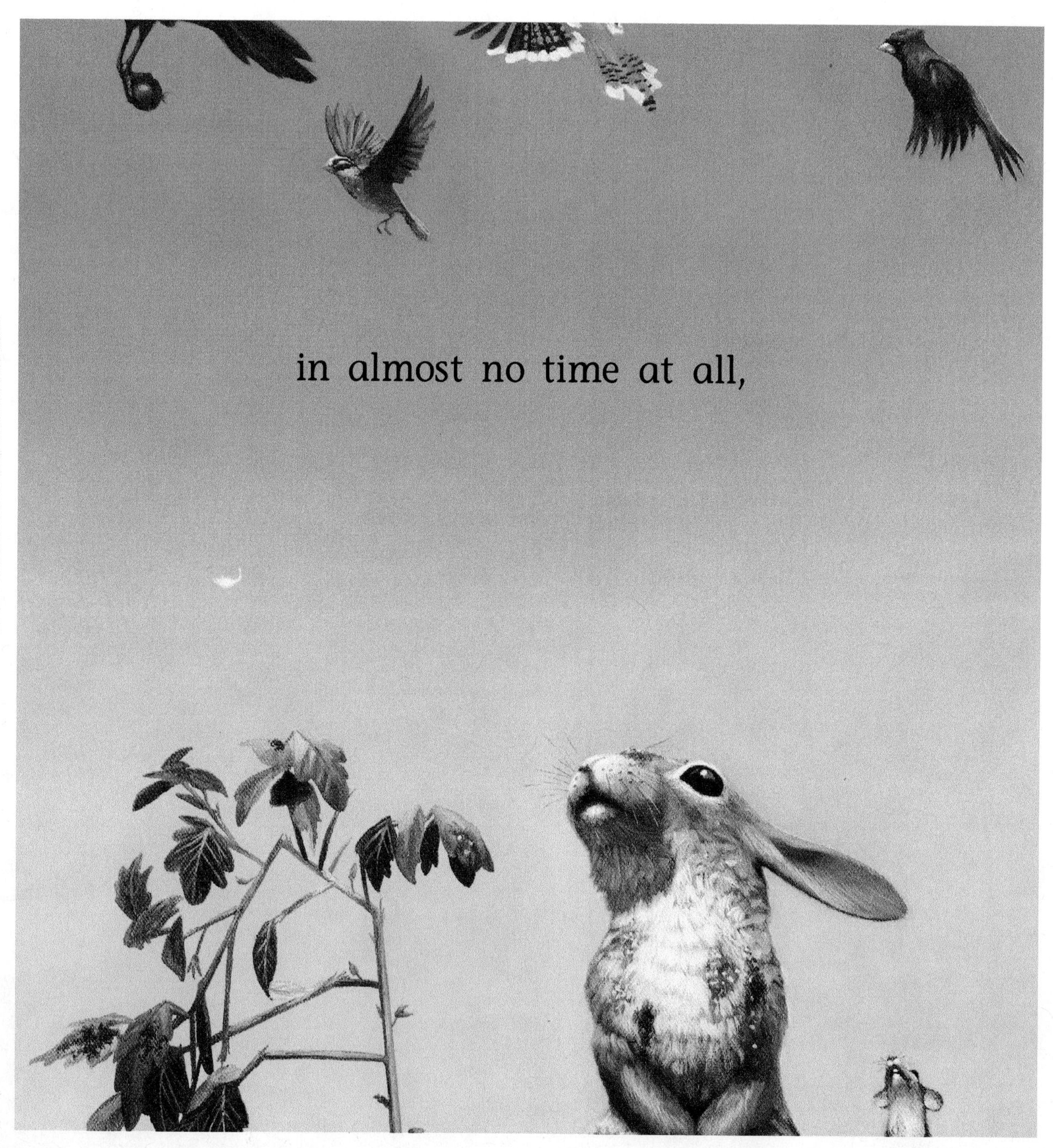

READ FOR UNDERSTANDING

ASK: Why do you think the rabbit and the mouse are staring at the birds? *(They are wondering what the birds are going to do.)*

FOLLOW-UP: What do you think they will do? *(Accept reasonable responses.)*

DOK 2

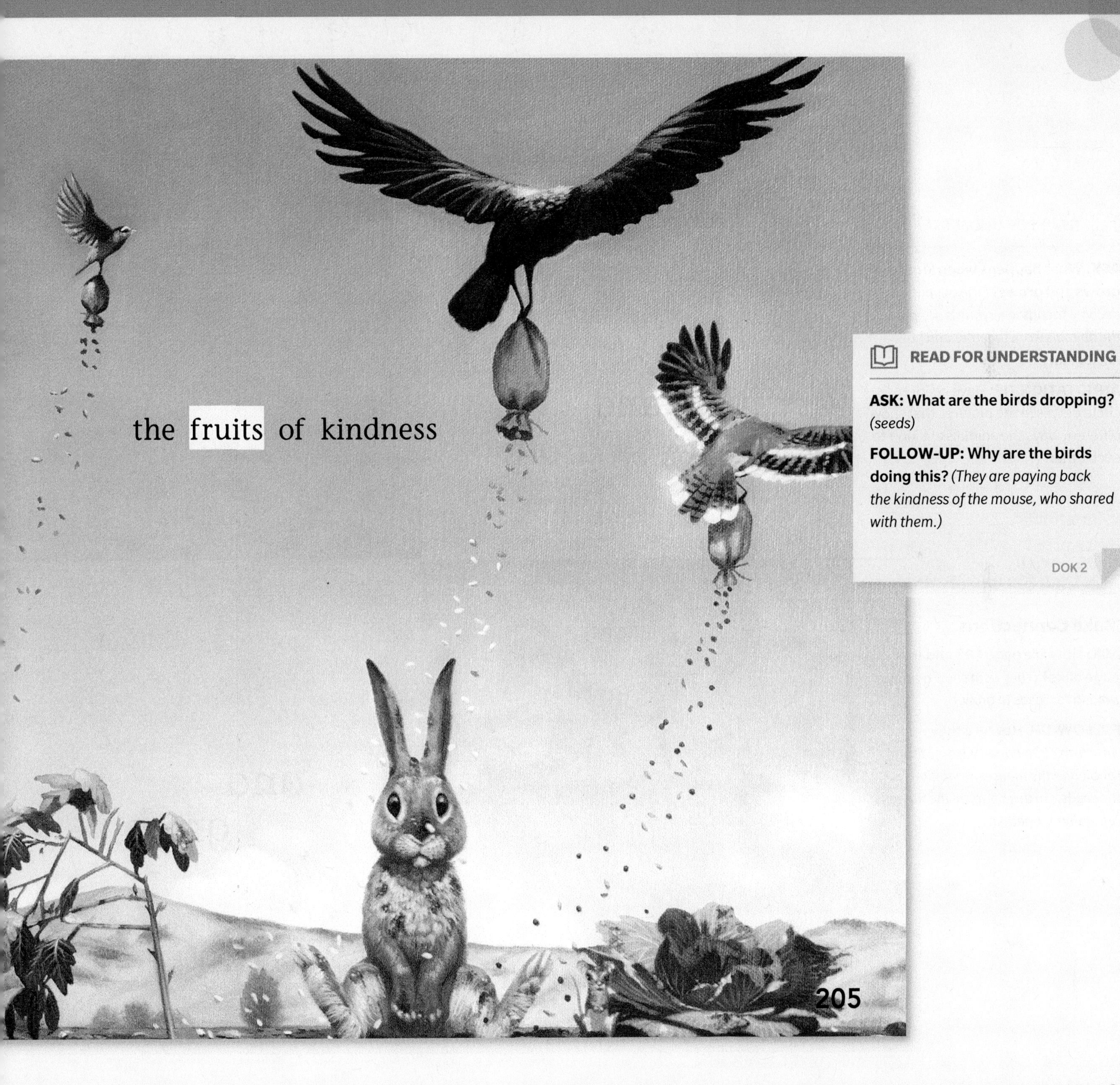

READ FOR UNDERSTANDING

ASK: What are the birds dropping? *(seeds)*

FOLLOW-UP: Why are the birds doing this? *(They are paying back the kindness of the mouse, who shared with them.)*

DOK 2

will

grow,

READ FOR UNDERSTANDING

ASK: What happens when kindness grows and grows? *(The animals become friends; everyone is happy; the animals work together and have fun together.)*

ANNOTATION TIP: Have children circle details in the pictures that show different ways the animals are kind to each other.

DOK 2

and

grow,

READ FOR UNDERSTANDING

Make Connections

ASK: How are page 193 and this page alike? *(They both show animals waiting for seeds to grow.)*

FOLLOW-UP: How are they different? *(On page 193, only the rabbit and the mouse are waiting for the seeds. On this page, all the friends are waiting together.)*

DOK 3

and

grow,

READ FOR UNDERSTANDING

Make Connections

MODEL MAKING A CONNECTION

THINK ALOUD *This reminds me of the story we read called* A Big Guy Took My Ball! *In both stories the characters do nice things for each other.*

DOK 3

READ FOR UNDERSTANDING

Phonics / Decoding in Context

Have children point to the word *sweet*. Review how the letters *sw* can be said close together so that they almost make one sound. **Model blending** the sounds in the word: /s/ /w/ /ē/ /t/, *sweet*. Have children repeat.

READ FOR UNDERSTANDING

Wrap Up

Revisit the predictions children made before reading. Have them confirm or correct their predictions using evidence from the text and pictures.

DOK 2

Respond to Reading

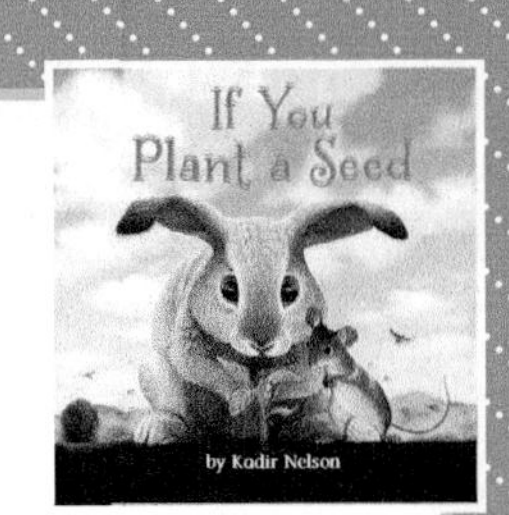

Use details from **If You Plant a Seed** to answer these questions with a partner.

1. **Make Connections** Think about what happens to all the friends in this story. How is this like what happens to the friends in **A Big Guy Took My Ball**?

2. What do the characters do to be kind?

Listening Tip

Listen carefully. Look at your partner to show that you are paying attention.

Academic Discussion

Use the TURN AND TALK routine. Remind children to follow agreed-upon rules for discussion, such as taking turns, listening carefully, and looking at their partner as he or she speaks.

Possible responses:

1. *The friends in both stories realize that being nice is a lot better than being afraid of or mean to each other.* DOK 3
2. *They share and work or play together.* DOK 3

Cite Text Evidence

READ Together

Write a Book Report

PROMPT What lesson did you learn from **If You Plant a Seed**? Write a book report to tell others about the story and how you feel about it.

PLAN First, write about the lesson you learned. Write what you like and do not like about the story.

Lesson	I Like	I Do Not Like

Write About Reading

- **Read aloud** the prompt.
- **Lead a discussion** in which children share their opinions about the lesson they learned from reading the story. Tell them to use text evidence to support their ideas.
- Then read aloud the Plan section. Have children use ideas from the discussion in their charts.

DOK 3

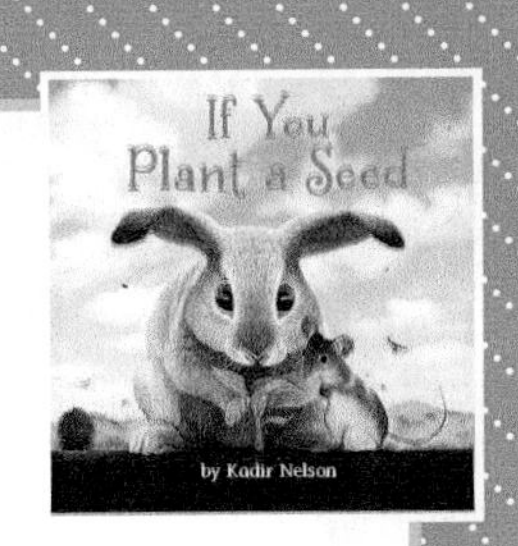

WRITE Now write your book report. First, tell the title. Tell about the lesson you learned. Then tell what you like or do not like. Use another sheet of paper if you need it. Remember to:

- Use the story for ideas.
- Give reasons for your opinions.

Responses may vary.

Write About Reading

- **Read aloud** the Write section.
- **Guide children** to state their opinion clearly and use the word *because* to explain their reasons.

DOK 3

Independent Close Reading

Have children close read and annotate "Fox and Crow" on their own during small-group or independent work time. As needed, **use the Scaffolded Support notes** that follow to guide children who need additional help.

Scaffolded Support

As needed, remind children to:

- make connections to their own experiences, to society, and to other texts they have read.
- think about the topic and look for clues that help them identify the theme.

DOK 3

Prepare to Read

GENRE STUDY **Fantasy** stories have made-up events that could not really happen.

MAKE A PREDICTION Preview **Fox and Crow**. Fox and Crow invite each other over for a meal. What do you think will happen?

They will eat food and have fun.

SET A PURPOSE Read to find out what happens when Fox and Crow eat together. Find out if your prediction is right.

212

Fox and Crow

READ What does Crow do that Fox does not like? Underline it.

One day, I asked Fox to eat a snack with me. Fox said "Yes!" My plan was to have a little fun with Fox. When he got to my nest, I set out seeds to eat. Just seeds. Fox was quiet. Then he said, "Crow, I am not a bird! I don't eat seeds! I am out of here!" ▶

Close Reading Tip

Put a ! by a surprising part.

CHECK MY UNDERSTANDING

When have you felt like Fox feels?

Responses will vary.

213

Scaffolded Support

As needed, remind children that:

- they can look for details in the words and pictures to help them understand how a character feels.
- something surprising could be a character acting in a way that is different from how it has acted before.

DOK 2

READ Who tells this part of the story? How do you know?

Crow made me mad, but she is still my friend. I asked her to eat with me. Soon Crow got to my den. I set out seeds for her to eat. I set out cookies for me.

"Fox, you have seeds for me!" Crow said. "How kind of you! Thank you. You are such a good friend! I am sorry that I was not kind to you before."

Close Reading Tip

Write C when you make a connection.

Scaffolded Support

As needed, remind children that:

- there may be more than one narrator in a story.
- they can use clues in the text and pictures to figure out the lesson that the author wants them to learn.
- when they make connections, they find ways that the text is like and unlike things in their own lives, another text, or their community.

DOK 3

CHECK MY UNDERSTANDING

What lesson about kindness do you learn from this story?

It is better to be kind to friends than to trick them.

Cite Text Evidence

WRITE ABOUT IT How are the things that happen in **Fox and Crow** like what happens in **If You Plant a Seed**? Write to explain. Use ideas from both stories.

In both stories, characters learn a lesson. Someone is mean at first, and others get mad. Then someone is kind, and everyone is happy.

215

Scaffolded Support

As needed, guide children to review both *If You Plant a Seed* and *Fox and Crow* before they begin writing and make notes about the things that are the same and different in the two stories. Have them use the notes as a guide to their writing.

DOK 3

VIEW FOR UNDERSTANDING

Introduce the Video

- **Read aloud** and discuss the information about the genre.
- **Guide children** to set a purpose for viewing to practice identifying the central idea.
- **Provide information** about the background topic, Kindness.

Prepare to View

GENRE STUDY **Videos** are short movies. Some videos give information. Others are for you to watch for enjoyment. Watch and listen for:

- how pictures and sounds work together
- how the video makes you feel
- a lesson you can learn

SET A PURPOSE Watch the video to find out what **central idea**, or important message, it shares. Look for details that help you understand it.

Build Background: Kindness

216

COLOR Your World with Kindness

from BetterWorldians Foundation

VIEW FOR UNDERSTANDING

Make Predictions

- **Display** the cover of *Color Your World with Kindness* for children.
- Have them **use prior knowledge** and the opening picture to predict what the video will be about. Tell children they will **return to their predictions** after they finish watching the video.

DOK 2

As You View Notice when the pictures change from gray to color. What happens each time one person helps another? Use details like these to figure out what the main message of the video is. How would you say this central idea in your own words?

VIEW FOR UNDERSTANDING

Central Idea

ASK: What is this video mostly about? *(kindness)*

FOLLOW-UP: Why do you think the author wanted to tell about why it is important to be kind to others? *(When one person is kind to another, that person is kind to someone else. Everyone is happier.)*

DOK 3

Respond to Media

READ Together

Use details from **Color Your World with Kindness** to answer these questions with a partner.

1. **Central Idea** What is the central idea you learn about kindness? Use details from the video to explain.

2. Describe the ways the people in the video help each other.

Talking Tip

Add on to what your partner says.

My idea is ______________.

Academic Discussion

Use the TURN AND TALK routine. Remind children to listen carefully to what others have to say about the topic and to build on their ideas.

Possible responses:

1. *People can make a difference in the world by being kind. The video shows one person being kind to another one, then that person being nice to another one.* DOK 3
2. *A boy shares an apple, a girl returns lost money, a man helps a woman with her bag, and a woman helps a child stop crying.* DOK 2

Revisit the Essential Question

- **Read aloud** the Essential Question.
- **Remind children** that in this module, they read different texts about being good citizens that can help them answer the question.
- **Have children** choose one of the activities to show what they learned in this module.

Character Remix

- **Encourage children** to make a list of the characters from the module's texts before deciding which two they will write about.
- **Challenge children** to write a line of dialogue for each character.

DOK 2

Let's Wrap Up!

Essential Question

Why is it important to do my best and get along with others?

Pick one of these activities to show what you have learned about the topic.

1. Character Remix

Pick two characters from two different texts you read. Imagine that they meet. Draw a picture of them working together or being kind to each other. Write about your picture.

2. Dear Good Citizen

Write a letter to the character you read about who you think is the best citizen. Give reasons why he or she is the best. Read your letter to a partner. Talk about it.

Word Challenge

Can you use the word courtesy to help explain one of your reasons?

My Notes

221

Dear Good Citizen

- **Review with children** the traits of a good citizen, based on what they learned from the texts in the module. Encourage them to think about those traits as they choose a character to write about.
- **Encourage children** to use the word *courtesy* in their letter.

DOK 2

Brainstorm and Plan

Have children use the My Notes space to jot down ideas for their chosen activity. Remind them to refer back to their notes as they complete the activity.

Glossary

body

camouflage

B

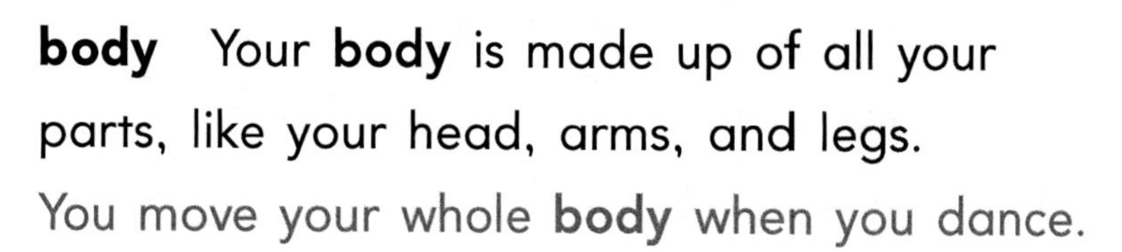

body Your **body** is made up of all your parts, like your head, arms, and legs.
You move your whole **body** when you dance.

C

camouflage **Camouflage** is what hides something or makes it difficult to see.
The animal's tan fur and spots are its **camouflage** in the grass.

characteristics **Characteristics** are things that make a person, animal, or thing different from others.
Short tails and long ears are **characteristics** of rabbits.

222

circling If you are **circling** something, you keep moving around it in a circle.
A bird was **circling** its nest before it landed in it.

coach If you **coach** people, you tell and show them how to do something.
My dad likes to **coach** my soccer team.

courtesy If you do something as a **courtesy**, you do it to be kind or polite.
He had the **courtesy** to help his grandma when it was raining.

courtesy

D

dull When something is **dull**, it is not bright.
It was a cloudy, **dull** day.

dull

223

E

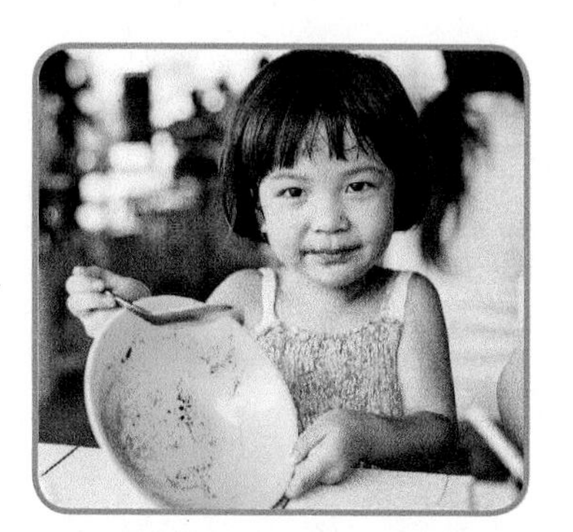
empty

empty If something is **empty,** it does not have anything in it.
I ate all my food, and now my bowl is **empty**.

equipment

equipment Your **equipment** is the stuff you need to play a game or do a job.
We need helmets and other **equipment** to play football.

exclaimed If someone **exclaimed** something, it was said in an excited way.
"Hooray!" the team **exclaimed** when they won.

excuse If you say "**excuse** me," it is a polite way to get someone's attention.
She said "**excuse** me" before she asked us a question.

224

exercise When you **exercise**, you move your body to get strong and healthy.
We **exercise** when we ride our bikes.

exercise

F

fan If you are a **fan** of something, you like it very much.
I cheer for the team since I am a big **fan**.

fan

fruits The **fruits** of something are the good things that come from it.
The **fruits** of trying hard are learning new things and feeling proud.

G

goal When you get a **goal** in a game, you get one or more points.
I scored one **goal** in the game.

225

guy

guy A **guy** is a man or boy.
A **guy** named Joe drives the school bus.

H

heap A **heap** is a lot of something.
I have a **heap** of work to do today.

herd When you **herd** animals, you make them move together into a group.
They **herd** the sheep into the barn.

hero

hero A **hero** is a person who does something brave to help others.
The man who saved the boy is a **hero**.

226

honest If you are an **honest** person, you tell the truth.
She was **honest** and told her mom she broke the cup.

honest

M

mammal A **mammal** is a kind of animal that has hair and feeds milk to its babies.
A whale is a **mammal**, and so are cats and people.

mammal

O

once If you do something **once** another thing happens, you do it right after.
I will do my homework **once** I finish eating.

227

predators

prey

P

predators **Predators** are animals that hunt other animals for food.
Little fish swim away from **predators** that want to eat them.

prey An animal that is hunted by other animals is the **prey**.
Fish are a bear's **prey**.

R

rules **Rules** tell what you can and cannot do.
We follow the **rules** when we play tag.

228

S

school A big group of fish that swims together is called a **school**.
A big **school** of fish swam by our boat.

seed A **seed** is a small, hard part of a plant that grows into a new plant.
A flower grew from the **seed** I planted in the dirt.

shingle A **shingle** is a small, flat piece of wood, or something else, used to cover a roof.
A big wind blew a **shingle** off our roof.

short A **short** time is a small amount of time.
We only waited a **short** time for the bus to come.

school

seed

229

shriek A **shriek** is a short, loud sound.
I made a loud **shriek** when I saw a snake.

soon If something will happen **soon**, it will happen a short time from now.
School is over, so we will be home **soon**.

sport A good **sport** plays fair and gets along with others.
He is a good **sport** and has fun even if he loses.

stroll When you take a **stroll**, you go on a slow walk.
We took a **stroll** through the park.

surprise A **surprise** is something you did not know you would see or do.
The pet that Mom and Dad gave us was a big **surprise**!

sport

surprise

T

team A **team** is a group of people who play a game against another group.
Our **team** won the game today!

thank You **thank** people when they do something nice for you.
I will **thank** him for the gift he gave me.

trouble **Trouble** is a problem or something that is hard to fix.
We had **trouble** finding our lost dog.

twigs **Twigs** are small, thin branches from a tree or bush.
The bird will build its nest with **twigs** from the tree.

team

twigs

231

warm

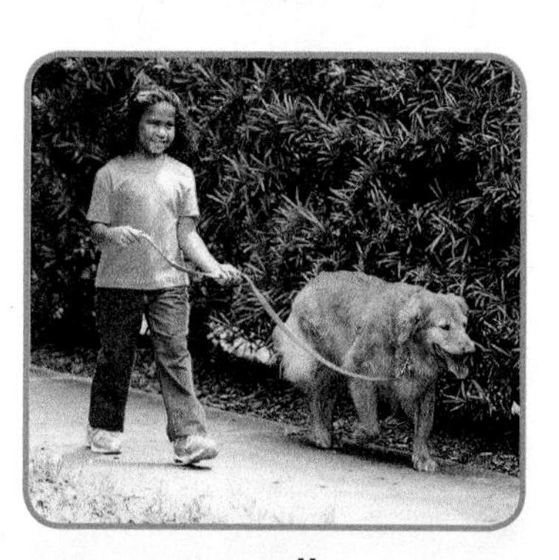
well

W

warm If something is **warm**, it is a little bit hot.

I feel **warm** when I wear my hat and coat.

well If you are **well**, you are healthy.

I feel **well** after I go for a long walk.

232

Index of Titles and Authors

233

Acknowledgments

A Big Guy Took My Ball! by Mo Willems. Copyright © 2013 by Mo Willems. Reprinted by permission of Disney Publishing Worldwide and Wernick & Pratt Agency.

Have You Heard the Nesting Bird? by Rita Gray, illustrated by Kenard Pak. Text copyright © 2014 by Rita Gray. Illustration copyright © 2014 by Kenard Pak. Reprinted by permission of Houghton Mifflin Harcourt Publishing Company.

"How to Defend Yourself Like an Armadillo," "How to Spin a Web Like a Spider," and "How to Trap Fish Like a Humpback Whale" from *How to Swallow a Pig* by Steve Jenkins and Robin Page. Copyright © 2015 by Houghton Mifflin Harcourt. Reprinted by permission of Houghton Mifflin Harcourt Publishing Company.

If You Plant a Seed by Kadir Nelson. Copyright © 2015 by Kadir Nelson. Reprinted by permission of HarperCollins Publishers.

Credits

4 (top penguin) ©flammulated/iStock/Getty Images Plus/Getty Images, (top elephant) ©Guenter Fischer/Getty Images, (top bat) ©Flickr/Ewen Charlton/Getty Images, (top turtle) ©Karel Gallas/Shutterstock; 5 (b) ©UbjsP/Shutterstock; 6 (t) (bg) ©Willard/iStock/Getty Images Plus/Getty Images, (top girl) ©FatCamera/iStock/Getty Images Plus/Getty Images, (b) ©Blackout Concepts/Alamy; 7 (b) ©Better Worldians Foundation; 8 ©Sharon Haeger/Shutterstock; 9 ©StanislavBeloglazov/Shutterstock; 12 (tl) ©flammulated/iStock/Getty Images Plus/Getty Images, (bl) ©MikeCardUK/iStock/Getty Images Plus/Getty Images, (tr) ©Karel Gallas/Shutterstock, (br) ©Sean Wandzilak/Shutterstock; 13 (tl) ©Guenter Fischer/Getty Images, (bl) ©Remsberg Inc./Design Pics/Getty Images, (tr) ©Flickr/Ewen Charlton/Getty Images, (br) ©cowboy5437/iStock/Getty Images Plus/Getty Images; 14 ©Jim Ruther Nill; 38 ©James Bruchac; 56 Courtesy of Houghton Mifflin Harcourt; 78 (fg) ©Neirfy/Shutterstock, (c) ©Yulia_Malinovskaya/iStockPhoto.com, (bg) ©aboutsung/Shutterstock; 79 ©Brian Kushner/Alamy; 80 ©wwing/iStockPhoto.com; 82 Courtesy of Houghton Mifflin Harcourt; 100 (inset) ©Chase Dekker Wild-Life Images/Getty Images, (bg) ©UbjsP/Shutterstock; 101 (bg) ©UbjsP/Shutterstock, (fg) ©All For You/Shutterstock; 102 *Video still from Beaver Family* ©National Geographic Stock; 104 ©Bertrand Demee/Photographer's Choice/Getty Images; 105 ©Holly Kuchera/Shutterstock; 106 (r) ©Be Good/Shutterstock, (l) ©ImagesBazaar/Getty Images, (bg) ©Bimbim/Shutterstock; 107 (r) ©Patricia Doyle/Photographer's Choice/Getty Images, (cr) ©MidoSemsem/Shutterstock, (cl) ©Lane Oatey/Blue Jean Images/Getty Images, (l) ©Dmytro Zinkevych/Shutterstock; 110 (bg) ©Willard/iStock/Getty Images Plus/Getty Images, (bl) ©FatCamera/iStock/Getty Images Plus/Getty Images; 111 (tl) ©GagliardiImages/Shutterstock, (tr) ©Blend Images/Alamy Images; 112 ©Jane Medina; 130 (t) ©Kanan Shabanov/Shutterstock; 131 (tl) ©Andersen Ross/Media Bakery, (tr) ©Mladen Mitrinovic/Shutterstock; 132 ©Kiankhoon/iStockPhoto.com; 134 ©Cristian Mallery Williams; 135 ©Blackout Concepts/Alamy; 136 (b) ©FatCamera/iStockPhoto.com; 136, 137, 138 (t) ©Ivan Nikulin/Shutterstock; 137 (b) ©Sonya Etchison/Shutterstock; 138 (b) ©Monkey Business Images/iStockPhoto.com; 139 (l) ©monkeybusinessimages/iStockPhoto.com, (r) ©Ivan Nikulin/Shutterstock; 140 (b) ©skynesher/iStockPhoto.com, (t) ©Ivan Nikulin/Shutterstock; 141 (r) ©DenKuvaiev/iStockPhoto.com, (l) ©Ivan Nikulin/Shutterstock; 142 (bg) ©Getty Images, (l) ©Ivan Nikulin/Shutterstock; 143 (b) ©FatCamera/iStockPhoto.com, (t) ©Ivan Nikulin/Shutterstock; 144 (tc) ©Jim Erickson/Media Bakery, (tl) ©Don Mason/Getty Images, (tr) ©SHOTFILE/Alamy Images, (bl) ©DoublePHOTO studio/Shutterstock, (bc) ©warrengoldswain/iStockPhoto.com, (br) ©fakezzz/iStockPhoto.com, (cr) ©Blend Images/Alamy, (c) ©JHershPhotography/iStockPhoto.com, (cl) ©bradleym/iStockPhoto.com, (l) ©Ivan Nikulin/Shutterstock; 148 (bg) ©denisik11/iStockPhoto.com, (fg) ©iStockPhoto.com, (r) ©Rawpixel/iStockPhoto.com, (l) ©shapecharge/iStockPhoto.com; 150 (tr) ©Rawpixel/iStockPhoto.com, (tl) ©shapecharge/iStockPhoto.com; 216 ©Weekend Images Inc./Getty Images; 217–218 *Video still from Color Your World with Kindness* ©Better Worldians Foundation; 220 ©FatCamera/iStockPhoto.com; 221 ©Dragon Images/Shutterstock; 222 (t) ©Rubberball/Getty Images, (b) ©Jason Gallier/Alamy; 223 (b) ©Edgar Bullon/Shutterstock; 224 (t) ©Moment Open/Getty Images, (b) ©Comstock/Getty Images; 225 (b) ©ESB Professional/Shutterstock, (t) ©Monkey Business Images/Shutterstock; 226 (t) ©bikeriderlondon/Shutterstock, (b) ©SanchalRat/Shutterstock; 227 (b) ©Yann Hubert/Shutterstock, (t) ©Alfira/Shutterstock; 228 (t) ©CatPix-The Art of Nature/Moment/Getty Images, (b) ©giv58/Fotolia; 229 (t) ©Getty Images; 230 (b) ©vectorfusionart/Shutterstock, (t) ©YakobchukOlena/Shutterstock; 231 (b) ©William Leaman/Alamy, (t) ©Lucky Business/Shutterstock; 232 (t) ©LWA/Dann Tardif/Getty Images

234